Natural Wonders of
NEW JERSEY

—— SECOND EDITION ——

Exploring Wild and Scenic Places

HOPE GRUZLOVIC AND AMY CRADIC

COUNTRY ROADS PRESS
NTC/Contemporary Publishing Group

Library of Congress Cataloging-in-Publication Data

Gruzlovic, Hope.
    Natural wonders of New Jersey : exploring wild and scenic places / Hope
Gruzlovic and Amy Cradic. — 2nd ed.
      p.   cm. — (Natural wonders)
    Includes index.
    ISBN 0-658-00187-6
    1. New Jersey—Guidebooks.   2. Natural history—New Jersey—
Guidebooks.   3. Natural areas—New Jersey—Guidebooks.   4. Parks—
New Jersey—Guidebooks.   5. Botanical gardens—New Jersey—
Guidebooks.   I. Cradic, Amy.   II. Title.   III. Series.
F132.3.G78   1999
917.4904'43—dc21   98-41798
                                                CIP

Cover and interior design by Nick Panos
Cover photograph: Delaware Water Gap. Copyright © John McGrail / Panoramic
Images, Chicago, 1998
Interior illustrations and map copyright © Gigi Bayliss. Spot illustrations
copyright © Barbara Kelley
Picture research by Elizabeth Broadrup Lieberman

Published by Country Roads Press
A division of NTC/Contemporary Publishing Group, Inc.
4255 West Touhy Avenue, Lincolnwood (Chicago), Illinois 60646-1975 U.S.A.
Copyright © 1999, 1994 by Hope Gruzlovic and Amy Cradic
Printed in the United States of America
International Standard Book Number: 0-658-00187-6
99 00 01 02 03 04 ML 19 18 17 16 15 14 13 12 11 10 9 8 7 6 5 4 3 2 1

Other titles in the Natural Wonders series include:

Natural Wonders of Kentucky .
Natural Wonders of Michigan
Natural Wonders of New Hampshire
Natural Wonders of New York
Natural Wonders of Ohio
Natural Wonders of Tennessee

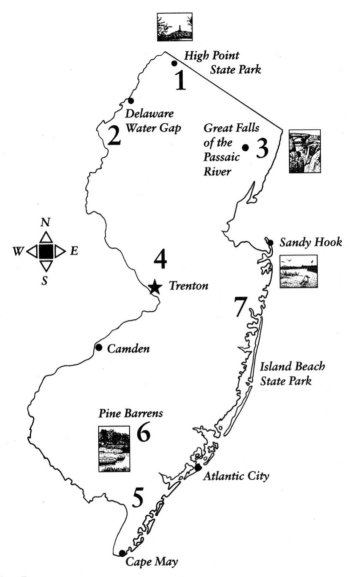

High Point
State Park

1

Delaware
Water Gap

2

Great Falls
of the
Passaic
River

3

Sandy Hook

N
W E
S

4

Trenton

7

Camden

Island Beach
State Park

Pine Barrens

6

Atlantic City

5

Cape May

New Jersey
(Figures correspond with chapter numbers.)

Contents

7   The Jersey Shore   105

Acknowledgments

Many people contributed to the preparation of this book. We owe particular thanks to the staffs of the New Jersey Division of Parks and Forestry and the Division of Fish, Game and Wildlife, who were always ready to share their expertise.

Introduction

Sitting atop Mount Tammany in the Delaware Water Gap, we watched hawks soar right in front of us and were struck by the diversity New Jersey has to offer. Just the weekend before, we were hiking through the pitch-pine forests of the Pine Barrens. Not long before that, we visited the Jersey Shore, where we watched bottle-nosed dolphins arcing up out of the ocean. We had spent months exploring natural wonders all across the state, yet still felt as though we had only scratched the surface.

New Jersey offers many different bridges to its natural world. Snug in your sleeping bag at Stokes State Forest, you can gaze from the darkness at the brilliant night sky and then learn more about the solar system at the State Museum's Planetarium. You can marvel at the graceful wading birds at the Edwin B. Forsythe Wildlife Refuge and then visit the Wetlands Institute to learn why such wetlands are essential to the survival of many of the state's endangered species.

In the following chapters, we've provided a sampling of places where you can both appreciate and learn about New Jersey's natural environment. If we are to preserve it for future generations, we must not only enjoy it, but protect it.

To simplify road designations, we've used the following abbreviations: I = Interstate; U.S. = U.S. Route or Highway; State = State Route or Highway; County = County Route or Highway.

1

Skylands Region

High Point State Park

It's hard to imagine a team of sled dogs racing along snow-covered trails any place other than Alaska or the frozen Yukon, but during the winter, if there is snow on the ground, members of the New Jersey Sled Dog Club can be found racing along the trails of High Point State Park.

But at 1,803 feet—the highest point in New Jersey—this park is bound to be colder than the rest of the state.

Located in the extreme northwest corner of the state, High Point lies along the Kittatinny Mountains in Sussex County and extends to the New York state line, joining Stokes State Forest to the south. The surrounding rugged terrain of the Kittatinny Mountains and the colder temperatures make High Point State Park an ideal place for winter activities. Cross-country skiing, snowmobiling, and dogsledding are common on weekends. Park rangers sometimes can be seen after a heavy snowfall patrolling the park on snowshoes.

The historic High Point Monument dominates the summit, and by climbing the monument's spiraling stairs to the top, visitors can witness the spectacular views of this more than 14,000-acre park.

High Point State Park

The park's surrounding natural beauty includes the cool, clear waters of Lake Marcia, winding trails, rich forest, and the more than 800 acres of the Dryden Kuser Natural Area. From the 220-foot height of the monument, standing as a memorial to New Jersey's wartime heroes, you can take in an amazing panoramic view of the surrounding mountains and countrysides of three states.

Westward across the Delaware River is an impressive view of Pennsylvania's Pocono Mountains, while looking to the north you can see the Catskill Mountains of New York. Just 40 miles to the southwest is New Jersey's Delaware Water Gap, and you can see the scenic Sunrise Mountain in Stokes State Forest, situated on the Kittatinny Ridge.

One of the most picturesque settings of the park is the Dryden Kuser Natural Area, which was dedicated in 1965 and named for New Jersey state senator and conservationist Dryden Kuser. The natural area includes a distinctive bog, known locally as the cedar swamp. A hiking trail along a ridge overlooking the cedar swamp circles the area, which is rich with large hemlocks, white pine, black spruce, and an unusual stand of mature southern white cedar not normally found at the 1,500-foot level of the bog. A trail guide, available at the park office, describes the spring and summer vegetation and other features of the surrounding area.

The swamp area was once a glacial lake formed during the end of the last Ice Age. Eventually, the waters were filled in with organic matter to form the bog that presently sits nestled in this mountainous region. This northernmost bog in New Jersey is known for its diverse plant life, including wild calla, goldthreads, witch hazel, and the insect-eating pitcher plants and sundews. In the winter, many of the park's wildlife migrate to the cedar swamp, which is protected from direct winds and heavy snow accumulation by the dense cedar trees and sheltered location.

Common mammals seen in the park include bats, voles, shrews, foxes, raccoon, beaver, woodchucks, and white-tailed deer. Several black bear dens also are known to exist in the park, where sightings of both adults and cubs are common in campsites.

Ten marked trails allow hikers to explore the park, ranging from difficult rocky terrain for experienced hikers to paths for casual walkers. The Monument Trail carries you uphill for a fair amount of time but also rewards you with numerous scenic views along the way. The trail also carries you past the cedar swamp and eventually back to the park's monument where it originates.

The Steenykill Trail is an especially scenic route from Lake Steenykill to the top of the High Point Mountain. If you're quiet, you might catch a glimpse of a beaver working not far from the lakeshore.

Several miles of the Appalachian Trail also run through the park, entering from the adjacent Stokes State Forest. The

Appalachian Trail extends for 2,100 miles from Georgia to Maine along the Appalachian Mountain Range. It is clearly marked by white blazes on trees. The 70 miles of the trail in New Jersey are located entirely on public land. The trail follows the Kittatinny Ridge from the Delaware Water Gap to near the New York–New Jersey border in High Point. The trail then turns eastward, following the state border until it exits the state west of Greenwood Lake.

Where: High Point State Park is located northwest of the town of Sussex, where it is readily accessible from State Route 23.

Hours: The park is open daily from sunrise to sunset. The park office is open Friday and Saturday from 9:00 A.M. to 8:00 P.M. during the summer and on weekdays year-round from 9:00 A.M. to 4:00 P.M.

Admission: $7.00 vehicle fee on weekends and holidays, $5.00 fee on weekdays charged at the park entrance from Memorial Day weekend through Labor Day.

Best time to visit: Year-round.

Activities: Swimming, picnicking, boating, camping, cross-country skiing, snowmobiling, mountain biking, and fishing are permitted. There are 50 family campsites in a secluded area of Sawmill Lake. The campsites, which cost $10.00 per night, have flush toilets. Two family cabins, each accommodating up to six people, are located along the shore of Steenykill Lake. A group cabin accommodating 28 people is also available. The cabins are open from May 15 through October 15. For reservations, contact the park office.

Concessions: A refreshment concession is located in the bathhouse at Lake Marcia.

Other: Only electric boats are permitted in the park, and pets are prohibited in all overnight facilities. The cabins, beach, and bathhouse are all wheelchair-accessible.

For more information: High Point State Park, 1480 State 23, Sussex, NJ 07461. Call 973-875-4800.

Note for State Park Visitors

Water, electric, and sewer hookups are not provided for trailers at any of New Jersey's state park and forest campgrounds. Pets are prohibited in overnight facilities. Visitors at overnight facilities are permitted between the hours of 8:00 A.M and 8:00 P.M. only.

Firewood is not furnished; however, some areas sell it. Fires are restricted to forest or park stoves and/or ground fireplaces, or to approved stoves provided by the camper. A limited number of campsites and lean-tos are open all winter, so check with the area office to determine the availability at specific campgrounds.

New Jersey State Park passes are available for $35.00 from park offices. This pass permits free parking at 22 areas that charge daily parking fees.

Stokes State Forest

From the narrow depths of Tillman Ravine to the sweeping overlook on Sunrise Mountain, you'll find plenty to explore in this 15,482-acre state park in Sussex County.

Located along 12 miles of the Kittatinny Mountain Ridge, Stokes features an extensive system of two dozen trails, including a 12.5-mile portion of the Appalachian Trail.

The forest, which lies in a transition zone where the central forest formation of oak and hickory overlaps and begins to give way to the northern formation of beech, birch, maple, and hemlock, is well known for its spectacular fall colors.

With woodland streams, lakes, ridges, and open spaces, Stokes provides a variety of wildlife habitats that attract everything from snakes and porcupines to migrating birds. The loose rocks, ledges, and rock outcroppings along the Kittatinny Ridge provide den sites for hibernating snakes, such as the copperhead and eastern rattlesnake. Thousands of migrating hawks and geese can be seen in the fall from Sunrise Mountain. In the valley regions, shallow beaver ponds along the Big Flatbrook and its tributaries attract flycatchers, herons, and woodpeckers, while the woods provide shelter for the black bear, bobcat, white-tailed deer, rabbits, wild turkey, and many species of woodland birds.

Spring is an especially nice time to visit. Flowering dogwood and azalea burst into full bloom, brightly colored wood warblers and other songbirds pass through or arrive to stay for the summer, and the brown, barren woodlands become leafy green. Trailing arbutus, Juneberry, lupine, rhododendron, wild violets, and other wildflowers add color to the forest floor, while higher up, mountain laurel blooms with white and pink flowers.

Tillman Ravine, in the southwestern portion of Stokes, is one of the most popular places to visit in any season. Here, the mountain stream known as Tillman Brook cuts through rock formations of metamorphosed red shale and sandstone, creating small waterfalls. Along the steep slopes on either side of the brook is an evergreen hemlock forest.

You'll see the access road to Tillman Ravine as you travel north of the visitors center on U.S. 206. Make a left onto Struble Road at the 4-H sign and follow this road for 4.5 miles to the first of two small parking lots. From this lot or the one farther up the road, you can begin a self-guided tour of a little more than half a mile, or 45 minutes of easy hiking. The trail loops around and will take you back to your starting point.

Tillman Brook rises in a spring along the side of the Kittatinny Mountains about 1.5 miles east of here. Formed by stream erosion, Tillman Ravine is relatively young, geologically speaking. Rapid removal of material by erosion has given the valley a V shape, which is characteristic of a youthful stream. In time, the deep valley will be eroded to a broad, gentle valley that is characteristic of a mature stream.

A favorite spot for many visitors is near the bottom of the ravine at what is known as the "teacup." The teacup is a large bowl formed by the swirling motion of sand and rock carried by rapidly moving water from the falls above. The swirling motion has a scouring effect, deepening and enlarging the bowl and giving it a circular shape and smooth walls. Eventually, the front wall of the bowl will be worn away and the falls will move upstream a little.

For now, the teacup resembles a large, circular bathtub. While it is only a few feet deep and swimming is not permitted, you can rest beside it, listen to the rushing falls, and soak your tired feet after a day of hiking, which is just what we did.

While the cool, moist climate of the ravine makes it a refreshing place to visit on warmer days, the beautiful ice formations that occur when the flowing water freezes in Tillman Brook give you a reason to return in the winter. From December 15 through March 15, however, you'll have to park at the 4-H parking lot on Struble Road and walk the remaining two miles into the ravine, since this section of the road is closed.

The crest of Sunrise Mountain, at an elevation of 1,653 feet above sea level, can be reached by hiking a section of the Appalachian Trail or by driving up Sunrise Mountain Road to the overlook parking lot. To get to this road, take Upper North Shore Road off U.S. 206, about one mile south of the park office. No matter how you get there, you'll be rewarded with a spectacular view of the farms and foothills below, with the Highlands of New Jersey to the east and the Pocono Plateau of Pennsylvania to the west. A pavilion and parking lot are at the summit.

If you decide to hike, you can park your car at the Culvers Gap parking area off Sunrise Mountain Road. From here, it's a rigorous five-mile, or three-hour, hike to the summit over a narrow and sometimes very rocky section of the white-blazed Appalachian Trail. For a shorter hike, you can drive part of the way up Sunrise Mountain Road, look for signs for the Appalachian Trail, park along the shoulder, and start hiking from there.

We chose to hike from Culvers Gap and found it to be quite a workout for occasional, not expert, hikers like us. But even though the trail was steep and rocky in many places, we managed to climb to the summit by making frequent rest stops. As you hike the trail, you may notice that some rocks appear to have grooves carved into them. These were caused by the movement of ice sheets 10,000 years ago when Sunrise Mountain was covered by several thousand feet of glacial ice.

When you finally make it to the scenic overlook at the top, you'll want to spend some time there, not just to recover from the hike, but to take in the panoramic view. During the fall, you can observe the annual hawk migration during which thousands of birds soar along the Kittatinny Ridge. Below, at the base of Sunrise Mountain, is New Jersey's largest rattlesnake den.

You also can reach the overlook by following the Tinsley Trail, which starts near the New Jersey School of Conservation within Stokes. To reach this trail, take U.S. 206 north from the park office for about two miles and take a right onto Flatbrook Road. Interesting glacial features along this trail include kettle holes—depressions formed when big ice blocks that had been trapped in sand, gravel, and rock melted—and huge rock ridges called moraines, which were left when the glacier retreated.

Where: Stokes State Forest is located five miles north of Branchville on U.S. 206.

Hours: The park office is open daily from 9:00 A.M. to 4:00 P.M.

Admission: $7.00 parking fee at Stony Lake on weekends and holidays and $5.00 on weekdays, Memorial Day weekend through Labor Day.

Best time to visit: Year-round.

Activities: Hiking, picnicking, cross-country skiing, and snowmobiling are permitted. Ice-skating is permitted on certain lakes within the forest; check with the office for information on safe conditions and use. Small boats with electric motors only are permitted on Lake Ocquittunk. Horseback riding and mountain biking are permitted on some trails. Stony Lake, which has a bathhouse and beach, is open for swimming from Memorial Day weekend through Labor Day weekend.

Concessions: Stony Lake has a food concession.

Pets: Pets are not permitted in campgrounds. Leashed dogs are permitted with visitors, but not on the beach.

Other: Maps and literature are available at the park office. Cabins (from $28.00 to $70.00 per night, depending on sleeping capacity) are in such demand here that a lottery is held annually to determine occupancy. Campsites are $10.00 with flush toilets, $8.00 without. Group campsites and lean-tos also are available.

For more information: Stokes State Forest, 1 Coursen Road, Branchville, NJ 07826. Call 973-948-3820.

Wawayanda State Park

Wawayanda State Park is a natural mosaic of upland swamp, rock outcrops, and lush forests located atop the Wawayanda Plateau. After several long but enjoyable days of hiking parts of the Appalachian Trail through New Jersey's Highlands, an early morning canoe ride on the 255-acre Wawayanda Lake offered a refreshing break for two tired hikers ready to sit back and enjoy the solitude of nature.

The dense hardwood forests that characterize the 13,422-acre state park provide a peaceful buffer for this pristine body of water, where canoeists and fishermen can escape from the hectic world and enjoy the captivating view of the surrounding northern Highlands.

We packed a bag lunch, rented a canoe, and set out in the early morning sunshine for the peaceful waters of the lake.

While canoeing, we found ourselves in the midst of dozens of honking, hungry geese. We also came upon a striking field of blooming lily pads decorating the water's surface from the northernmost shore of the lake. White and yellow blossoms, the trees, and early morning sky all reflected brilliantly on the water's surface.

Many species of game fish can be found in Lake Wawayanda and the smaller lakes of the park, offering anglers the choice of largemouth and smallmouth bass, perch, pickerel, and brown and rainbow trout. We saw several fishermen in boats and other canoes during our ride, but with such a wide expanse of water surrounding us in all directions, we seemed to spend most of our time lazily floating along in solitude with only an occasional passerby.

A boat rental facility and launching ramp are located near the Lake Wawayanda beach and picnic areas. Canoes, rowboats, kayaks, and paddleboats can be rented, and privately owned boats can be launched at no charge. Only electric boats are permitted.

The lake also has a designated white-sand beach bathing area open for swimming from Memorial Day weekend through Labor Day.

There is much more to explore in the park, aside from the picturesque setting of Lake Wawayanda. Almost one-third of Wawayanda State Park has been preserved through the State Natural Areas System. The three sections designated as natural areas are Bearfort Mountain, Hemlock Ravine, and Wawayanda Swamp.

Wawayanda Swamp Natural Area, the largest of the three, was recognized due to its globally rare inland Atlantic white cedar swamp, mixed oak hardwood forest, and glacially formed, spring-fed lake. You often can see beavers here from the bridge on the Double Pond Trail. The area has several other trails, including one short, scenic trail around the glacial lake of Laurel Pond.

Located in the southern portion of the park is Bearfort Mountain Natural Area. This 1,325-acre area is home to several birds on the state's threatened list, including the red-shouldered hawk and barred owl. The endangered timber rattlesnake and bog turtle also can be seen among the area's interspersed swamp hardwoods, scrub oak, rock outcrops, and oak hardwood forest.

Three plant species on the state's endangered list, the Dewey's sedge, white-grained mountain ricegrass, and witch hobble, can be seen in the Hemlock Ravine Natural Area. Although the Hemlock Ravine is small compared to the other two natural areas, it offers a cool, quiet place to rest during a day's hike.

In addition to the three natural areas, the Ferber Wildlife Sanctuary, established in 1982, is another area in which to enjoy the park's natural habitat.

A 19.6-mile portion of the Appalachian Trail follows the sometimes rocky terrain of Wawayanda Mountain and offers various views of the park's diverse landscape. An additional 40 miles of hiking trails throughout the park also offer the opportunity for both casual walkers and avid hikers to visit the park's natural features.

Along the northern shore of Wawayanda Lake are the remains of Double Pond, an old iron-smelting town operated during the late 19th century. A charcoal blast furnace still stands in the once-thriving village, which is reminiscent of industrial America.

Logged heavily during the 1940s, the park is laced with old logging roads that have been converted to trails. Fortunately, with the variety of endangered plant and wildlife species surviving in the natural habitat, the sounds of saws and falling trees that once echoed through the park have been replaced by the natural chatters and songs of wildlife.

Where: Wawayanda State Park is located along the New York border in Sussex and Passaic counties and can be entered from the east via Warwick Turnpike along the main entrance road. **Hours:** The park is open during daylight hours throughout the year. The visitors center is open from 8:00 A.M. to 4:00

P.M. on weekdays and from 8:00 A.M. to 4:30 P.M. on weekends and holidays. Winter hours may vary.

Admission: $7.00 parking fee on weekends and holidays, $5.00 on weekends charged at the park entrance from Memorial Day weekend through Labor Day.

Best time to visit: Year-round.

Activities: A number of winter activities, including cross-country skiing, ice-skating, ice fishing, snowshoeing, and snowmobiling, are permitted on designated trails and in various areas of the park. Mountain biking is also popular year-round. Three group campsites are available from April 1 through October 31, with a minimum of seven people per site. Reservations can be made through the mail or in person. For information on wheelchair access, contact the park office.

Concessions: A food concession is available to day-use visitors from Memorial Day weekend through Labor Day.

Other: Deer, grouse, squirrels, turkeys, rabbits, raccoons, and groundhogs can be hunted with bow and arrow, shotgun, and black powder firearms in their appropriate seasons.

For more information: Wawayanda State Park, P.O. Box 198, Highland Lakes, NJ 07422. Call 973-853-4462.

Sterling Hill Mine and Museum

The Franklin-Ogdensburg area of Sussex County is one of the richest mineral deposits in the world. More than 340 minerals, or 10 percent of all known species, can be found here. About 30 of these minerals are unique to this area.

Of prime economic importance to the area for more than 100 years were the rich zinc deposits that were mined at both Sterling Hill Mine and the nearby Franklin Mine. Two of the primary minerals from which the zinc was extracted— franklinite and zincite—are mined nowhere else in the world.

The Franklin Mine's supply of zinc was exhausted in 1954, but Sterling Hill continued its mining operations until 1986. Three years later, following a dispute between the New Jersey Zinc Company and the Borough of Ogdensburg, the borough took title to the Sterling property and auctioned it off. Two brothers, Richard and Robert Hauck, took title to the mine property in 1989 and, with the help of many volunteers—including ex-miners, geologists, mineral collectors, and former zinc company employees—worked to preserve this piece of mining history.

You can tour Sterling Hill, which was New Jersey's last operating underground mine, and learn about the history and process of mining by visiting this National Historic Site. Highlights of the tour include an aboveground exhibit hall, featuring more than 60 displays of mining equipment and other antiques, and the Rainbow Room, which is located underground. Here, with the help of ultraviolet lights, the gray rock walls of the mine glow with spectacular fluorescent colors.

The exhibit hall, an aboveground building near the museum's office, was used by miners as a changing and showering area. Inside each miner's locker was a chain that was attached to a wire basket overhead. Miners would put their wet, muddy clothes into the baskets at the end of each shift and haul them up toward the ceiling, where they would dry overnight. Today, on one side of the exhibit hall, their work clothes still hang from the ceiling as ghostly reminders of the past.

The Rainbow Room, located off a damp, earthen-smelling tunnel of the mine, is the high point of the underground tour, especially for children. A few seconds after the incandescent lights are turned off and the ultraviolet lights switched on, the gray, rock walls of the room suddenly glow with vibrant green, orange, red, blue, and purple. More than 70 fluorescent species of minerals have been found in the Franklin-Ogdensburg ore deposits.

What's nice about the tour is that it is unhurried. There's plenty of time to take in the wonder of the Rainbow Room, to enjoy the exhibits at your own pace, and to allow for plenty of questions. At a minimum, the tour takes an hour and a half, but usually it lasts about two hours. For that reason, it's not recommended for preschoolers who may have limited attention spans. Bring a sweater or jacket, because the underground temperature is in the mid-50s.

Except for December through February, when the museum is closed, the public is invited to explore the mine's mineral dump on the last Sunday of every month. For $10.00, you can take home 10 pounds of minerals. Fluorescent minerals are easily found by visitors with shortwave ultraviolet lights, and crystals also can be located. Museum representatives say it's not uncommon to leave with $100.00 worth of minerals for your $10. Children under 13 are not permitted.

Where: Sterling Hill Mine and Museum is located on Plant Street, Ogdensburg, Sussex County. From Franklin, take County 517 south three miles to Ogdensburg. In the center of Ogdensburg, turn right onto Passaic Avenue and follow signs to the mine.

Hours: Daily 10:00 A.M. to 5:00 P.M. The last tour is at 3:00 P.M. Closed December 1 through April 1, but open for tours from December 26 to 31 and on weekends in December and March, weather permitting.

Admission: $9.00 for adults, $8.00 for senior citizens, and $6.00 for children under 17.

Best time to visit: March through November.

Activities: You can hunt for minerals on the last Sunday of the month, from March through November, if you are 13 years of age or older.

Concessions: A snack stand in the main office is open on weekends and during peak periods. A museum shop sells books, souvenirs, and mineral specimens.

Other: The tour is less than a half mile of easy walking. Half the distance is outdoors. Be sure to bring a sweater or jacket. Picnic sites are available.

For more information: Sterling Hill Mine and Museum, 30 Plant Street, Ogdensburg, NJ 07439. Call 973-209-7212.

The Franklin Mineral Museum

While Sterling Hill Mine and Museum is devoted more to the history of mining, the nearby Franklin Mineral Museum is known for its extensive mineral collection of more than 300 species from the Franklin-Ogdensburg area.

Thousands of specimens are on display in the Franklin Mineral Museum's three rooms. The Fluorescent Room, where ores and minerals glow under ultraviolet light, is the most memorable. About 75 different types of fluorescent minerals can be found in this area, more than anywhere else. Since more are found at Franklin than at Sterling Hill, Franklin has earned the title of "Fluorescent Mineral Capital of the World."

Also on display in a new wing are natural history collections of fossils, Native American relics, rocks, and minerals. The fossils include fish, dinosaur footprints, shells, bones, skulls, and beautiful petrified wood. The Native American section features New Jersey finds, western beadwork, and pottery. A mineral display features more than 4,200 specimens from around the world.

You also can tour an aboveground replica mine here. Of particular interest to children is the Buckwheat Dump, where they can search for minerals and check out the colors in an ultraviolet booth. Unlike the Sterling Hill dump site, the

Buckwheat Dump is open whenever the Franklin Mineral Museum is open. The museum is located only three miles from the Sterling Hill Mine and Museum.

Where: The Franklin Mineral Museum is located off State 23 in Franklin; follow the blue signs.

Hours: Monday through Saturday from 10:00 A.M. to 4:00 P.M. and Sunday from 12:30 P.M. to 4:30 P.M. from March 1 through December 1 only. (Closed Easter and Thanksgiving.)

Admission: $4.00 for adults, $2.00 for preschool through high school students includes guided tours. There is a separate admission fee to go rock hunting in the Buckwheat Dump.

Concessions: A gift shop in the lobby sells minerals and related items, including ultraviolet mineral lamps.

Other: Picnic sites are available.

For more information: Franklin Mineral Museum, P.O. Box 54, Franklin, NJ 07416. Call 973-827-3481.

The Pequest Trout Hatchery and Natural Resource Education Center

Each year, the Pequest hatchery produces more than 600,000 brook, brown, and rainbow trout for stocking in more than 200 bodies of water that are open to public fishing. In fact, if you've ever caught a trout in New Jersey, chances are it was raised at Pequest. You can learn all about the fish-rearing process and about the importance of conserving our natural resources by paying a visit to this facility, operated by the New Jersey Division of Fish, Game and Wildlife.

The hatchery is located in the Pequest Wildlife Management Area, which encompasses more than 3,500 acres in the Pequest Valley in scenic Warren County. Below the surface is a large aquifer containing some of the purest water in New

Jersey. A network of six wells supplies up to 7,000 gallons of this water a minute to the hatchery at a consistent 50–52 degrees Fahrenheit year-round.

When entering Pequest's main building, you'll see an exhibit hall off to the right. This hall features several interactive exhibits designed to teach you about New Jersey's natural resources and how you can help to conserve them. One exhibit challenges you to figure out in which habitat a particular species belongs, while a computer across the room asks you to make decisions about environmental issues. There are a few trout in holding tanks in the exhibit area and in front of the building. For a quarter, an automatic dispenser will provide you with a handful of food so you can feed them.

Kids will have fun with the exhibits, while adults are sure to learn something new, too. A backyard wildlife area outside the exhibit hall, featuring bird feeders and berry-producing shrubs, shows how you can create a habitat that will attract birds and other wildlife right outside your own home.

Off to the left of the entrance is the auditorium, where a 15-minute, continuously running videotape explains the hatchery's operations. After watching it, follow the pattern of green fish on the sidewalk, which will lead you to the nursery and observation platform.

The fish-rearing process actually starts within the broodstock building, which is not open to the public. Here, 6,000 two- and three-year-old broodfish produce the hatchery's entire supply of eggs. In the fall, hatchery workers strip, or squeeze, the eggs from the broodfish and transfer them to the nursery building, where they are incubated in insulated trays. The eggs hatch in about 30 days into what are called sac fry, less than an inch long. Then they are transferred into rearing tanks where they are automatically fed and periodically sorted by size. If you visit from October through May, you can see them in the tanks through the nursery window.

By spring, these trout have reached fingerling size of three to four inches and are transferred to the more than one mile of concrete raceways outside, which you can view from the observation platform. Four times a day, usually at around 8:00 A.M., 11:00 A.M., 1:00 P.M., and 3:00 P.M., a truck releases food into the raceways. The food is a specially prepared formula in pellet form. If you're present at this time, you'll witness a true feeding frenzy. The trout remain in the raceways until the following spring, when they will average 10.5 inches long and be ready for stocking.

Where: The Pequest Trout Hatchery is located nine miles west of Hackettstown on U.S. 46.
Hours: Daily from 10:00 A.M. to 4:00 P.M., except for holidays.
Admission: Free.
Best time to visit: October through May (to see trout in nursery). Fish can be seen in raceways year-round.
Activities: Hiking trails, picnic grounds, and a fishing education pond used in special programs are located outside the facility. In addition, the 3,500-acre wildlife management area is open to fishing, hunting, hiking, bird-watching, and other wildlife-related recreation. Good overlook points provide hawk-watching opportunities in the fall.
Concessions: None.
Other: Special programs about fish, wildlife, and other natural resources are offered as part of the "Budding Naturalist" series. If you ask to be put on the mailing list, you'll receive a brochure three times a year that lists these activities. The hatchery is wheelchair-accessible, and fishing access for the disabled is located on the Pequest River near the entrance to the hatchery.
For more information: The New Jersey Division of Fish,

Game and Wildlife, 605 Pequest Road, Oxford, NJ 07863-9748. Call 908-637-4125.

Ken Lockwood Gorge Wildlife Management Area

The Ken Lockwood Gorge Wildlife Management Area in Hunterdon County is one of New Jersey's most picturesque wildlife management areas. About 2.5 miles of the South Branch of the Raritan River flow through this gorge, which is a popular fly-fishing spot from April through November. But you don't have to be a fisherman to appreciate its wild beauty. In fact, a visit here was one of our favorite day trips.

We hiked along this section of the South Branch one hot July morning, enjoying the cool shade of the tall hemlocks lining the steep slopes on either side of the river. Boulders are strewn throughout the river, with rapids, small waterfalls, and pools interspersed along the way. The easiest way to follow the river is by walking along the area's access road, which runs parallel to the water. If you want to explore the other side of the river, it's easy enough to find a downed tree or some strategically placed boulders that will allow you to cross.

This 260-acre wildlife management area is managed primarily for fishing. Hunters know the area for its many grouse, squirrel, and deer. Of the 10 species of fish that can be found here, the most abundant are the brook, brown, and rainbow trout; smallmouth bass; rock bass; and sunfish. Trout are stocked throughout the spring and in the fall. While you're enjoying the river, remember that you're sharing it with fishermen, who won't appreciate it if you splash into the water nearby. That doesn't mean, however, that you can't get close enough to appreciate the graceful casting that makes fly-fishing the true art that it is.

When driving into and out of the wildlife management area, you should exercise particular caution. The access road is unpaved and is marked by many potholes, requiring some careful steering. The road is narrow in some areas, so be prepared to back up or pull over if a vehicle approaches from the opposite direction. The road is considered impassable during the winter months.

Where: Ken Lockwood Gorge is located north of High Bridge and east of County 513 in Lebanon Township, Hunterdon County. From State 31, take County 513 past the entrance to Voorhees State Park. After mile marker 20, make a right onto Main Street (County 512 east). Cross the bridge and make an immediate right onto River Road. Continue straight into gorge.

Hours: Dusk to dawn daily.

Admission: Free.

Best time to visit: Spring and fall.

Activities: Hiking, photography, bird-watching, hunting, and fishing are popular.

Concessions: None.

Pets: Dogs are permitted, but a leash is recommended.

Other: Swimming, camping, and picnicking are not allowed.

For more information: The New Jersey Division of Fish, Game and Wildlife, P.O. Box 400, Trenton, NJ 08625-0400. Call 908-637-4125.

The George Griswold Frelinghuysen Arboretum

Some of the most alluring aspects of the Frelinghuysen Arboretum in Morris County are the small, intimate resting areas hidden beneath shade trees along the forested trails, the rolling green lawns stretching out from the steps of the arboretum's Colonial Revival estate, and the wide range of native and exotic plants in both formal and informal settings.

The 127-acre tract of the Frelinghuysen Arboretum attracts visitors in every season. Flowering cherries and rhododendrons bloom along with the azaleas in the spring. Peonies, roses, and annuals add brilliant color to hot summer days, while the fall brings color to oaks, maples, and sweet gums. Even in the winter, the garden hollies add brightness to the landscape.

The arboretum is especially well known for its spring lilac collection. The fragrant and colorful blooms of lilacs were particular favorites of the original residents, the George Griswold Frelinghuysen family. The family spent summers at the arboretum, which was originally known as Whippany Farm. Because theirs was a summer house, the Frelinghuysens favored flora that blossomed between April and May, such as the lilacs that still decorate the lawns today.

Whippany Farm was donated to the people of Morris County in 1969 by Mathilda E. Frelinghuysen, who had inherited the property from her parents and initiated the plans to convert her private estate into a public arboretum.

The elegant Frelinghuysen Mansion, an official historic site of the county, now serves as the administrative headquarters of the Morris County Park Commission. The arboretum itself is a regional center for a variety of horticultural activities, including education programs and a botanical library.

The arboretum features collections of trees and shrubs labeled for educational and scientific purposes. There are also two self-guided trails through the arboretum.

The red trail, the shorter of the two, begins and ends at the Haggerty Education Center, stopping at 28 stations along the way. You can follow the red marks along the paved walk that loops around the front lawn where a collection of Japanese maples stands. The trail takes about 50 minutes and affords you with such sights as the unusual purple-leafed sycamore maple, graceful English yews, and the Babbott Flowering Cherry Collection.

Located about halfway through the trail is the Margaret C. Oneil Knot Garden, a new addition to the arboretum, where carefully pruned plants form an intricate, intertwined design. Knot gardens were popular during the reign of the Tudors.

The blue trail also begins at the Haggerty Education Center, but ends at the nearby parking lot. With 61 stops in all, the blue trail covers a greater and more diverse area of the surrounding arboretum.

Some of the trail's highlights are the ornamental Helen Page Wodell Azalea Trail, the Riker Holly and Aldrich Dogwood Memorials, and the Elmer O. Lampi Shade Garden.

The shade garden is the perfect place to relax and enjoy the scenic sights. A small pool, a variety of flowering trees, shrubs, and ferns, and a collection of shade-thriving flowers, such as crested irises, Bethlehem sage, and showy sedums, lend the area a picturesque appearance.

There are numerous gardens apart from the trails that you can visit, including the Klipstein Blue Garden, the Mary Lindner Perennial Garden and Cottage Garden, and the Beth Fisher Winter Garden.

The unique Watnong Rock Garden is an especially scenic display. The garden features specific plants that often inhabit cliffs, moraines, or mountainous areas, such as campanulas, phlox, and sedums.

The Vera Scherer Garden was designed to teach people with disabilities about different methods and equipment that can make gardening more accessible to them. Flower beds, for example, are constructed to eliminate the bending and stretching of outside gardening, providing the option of standing or sitting in a wheelchair to work. This garden is planted, harvested, and maintained by special program participants under the guidance of staff and volunteers.

Besides the many horticultural activities offered in the park, "Branching Out!" a youth educational program cosponsored by the Friends of the Frelinghuysen Arboretum and the Morris County Park Commission, offers a special opportunity for children between the ages of seven and twelve to learn how to raise their own vegetables, herbs, and flowers. The program, which is offered only during the spring and summer, charges special fees. For more information, contact the Morris County Park Commission.

Where: The Frelinghuysen Arboretum is located off Exit 36A of I-287 north. Proceed in the center lane of Morris Avenue for approximately half a mile to Whippany Road. Continue to the second traffic light, making a left turn onto East Hanover Avenue. Travel approximately one-quarter mile to the entrance. From I-287 south, take Exit 36, following signs to Ridgedale Avenue. At Ridgedale Avenue, proceed until the first traffic light and make a right turn onto East Hanover Avenue.

Hours: The Haggerty Education Center is open from Monday through Saturday from 9:00 A.M. to 4:00 P.M. and on Sunday from noon to 4:30 P.M. The gardens are open from 8:00 A.M. until dusk.

Admission: Free. There is a fee for some programs.

Best time to visit: Spring and fall.

Activities: Horticultural classes, as well as other programs, are available for adults and children through the arboretum. "Branching Out!" is a hands-on, youth educational program cosponsored by the Friends of the Frelinghuysen Arboretum and the Morris County Park Commission.

Concessions: A gift shop is located near the main parking lot.

Other: The Joseph F. Haggerty Education Center, Braille Trail, and Home Demonstration Gardens are designed to expand the Morris County Park Commission's services to the gardening public in a barrier-free environment.

For more information: Morris County Park Commission, 53 East Hanover Avenue, P.O. Box 1295, Morristown, NJ 07962. Call 973-326-7600.

Hacklebarney State Park

Hacklebarney State Park is located along the Black River in a gorge of unusual beauty. The 873-acre natural area is primarily made up of glacial valley, within which lies a cool hemlock-and-boulder-lined ravine.

In the springtime, white-tipped water can be seen gushing down an eight- to ten-foot drop, landing in the cool waters of a brook. The air is filled with the scent of the park's many wildflowers, including pink lady's slipper, wild lily of the valley, and the rare ginseng with its white and purple blossoms.

We arrived early at the park on a warm, bright day and stopped by the ranger station before heading out to the trails. The ranger was just opening up the station and commented to us that, with such an early start, we had a good chance of catching a glimpse of some of the park's wildlife—particularly a black bear that had been seen in the park for the previous several weeks.

Bobcats, red and gray foxes, deer, travel packs of coyotes, possum, and wild turkey are some of the other wildlife that the ranger mentioned could be found in the park.

Well, we never did see that bear, but the trails that led us along the shaded hillsides and banks of the river were some of the most peaceful and breathtaking ones you'll find in New Jersey.

A large section of the trail that runs parallel to the river is pretty rugged. At times, we found ourselves climbing over and between huge boulders, where roots of tall hardwoods amazingly seemed to be planted in the terrain's thick black rock.

The Black River and its two tributary streams, Rinehart Brook and Trout Brook, are main attractions at the park. The Black River, the most popular fishing spot here, is stocked annually with brook, brown, and rainbow trout in April and May. Both Trout Brook and Rinehart Brook are designated wild trout streams, which are left unstocked to preserve natural spawning habitats.

The park was established in 1924 when Adolphe E. Borie donated 32 acres of land to the state as a memorial to his mother, Susan P. Borie, and his grandniece, Susan R. Patterson. Through state programs, donations, and capital purchases, the remaining acreage was acquired.

There are several stories as to how the park's name "Hacklebarney" originated. One story says the name came about because workmen from a nearby iron mine persisted in heckling a quick-tempered foreman, Barney Tracey. "Heckle" Barney, in time, became Hacklebarney.

The Lenni-Lenape Indians who inhabited the Hacklebarney area called the Black River the Allamatunk River, meaning "black rock" or "black earth bottom."

Indian corn, or "maize," made up a substantial part of the diet of these early hunters and gatherers. The women of the tribe used both hollowed-out tree trunks and large rocks along the river's edge to hold corn, which they ground into mush. From hundreds of years of grinding corn on these same rocks, deep indentations resulted. These rocks came to be called mushpots. A few mushpots remain alongside the Black River in the Hacklebarney area.

Many Native American artifacts have been discovered throughout northern New Jersey, including the surrounding areas of Hacklebarney State Park. These artifacts include thousands of arrowheads and hundreds of spears, tomahawks, axes, hoes, and grinding and polishing stones. Also found were pendants that Native Americans once wore around their necks to ward off evil spirits.

Picnic sites are located along the Trout Brook and the Black River. Access is by foot. Since the trails in the park can be rugged at times, it is a good idea to wear comfortable walking or hiking shoes.

Where: Hacklebarney State Park is located in Long Valley, about three miles southwest of Chester, with access from State 24, U.S. 206, and County 517.
Hours: Hours vary depending on the season. Call park headquarters.
Admission: No admission fee.
Best time to visit: This is a good place to observe the fall foliage.
Activities: Hiking, fishing, hunting, and picnicking are permitted. No regularly scheduled events are held at the park.
Other: Trail maps are available at the ranger station located adjacent to the main parking area. Trout are stocked in the spring and fall.
For more information: Hacklebarney State Park, c/o Voorhees State Park, 251 County Road 513, Glen Gardner, NJ 08826. Call 908-638-6969.

Well-Sweep Herb Farm

Whether you're a cook who likes to experiment with herbs or someone who just enjoys exploring the unusual, this farm is worth a visit. Owners Cyrus and Louise Hyde maintain the beautiful and fragrant herb gardens here on their large farm in Warren County.

The gardens include about 1,200 varieties of herbs and perennials. The formal herb garden, which is intended for educational purposes and has attracted visitors from around the world, includes more than 100 types of scented geraniums, more than 60 lavenders, about 60 types of rosemary, and 3 dozen basils.

The ideal time to visit is during a free open house held each year, usually in June. Guided lecture tours are offered through the herb gardens and around the farm. A summer herb festival, usually held in July, features a series of lectures on a variety of topics, ranging from edible flowers to making your own herb vinegars. Lunch is provided and an admission fee is charged.

If you're looking to buy herbs, the best time to visit is mid-May, when you'll have the best selection. The biggest sellers are the cooking herbs, such as oregano, thyme, basil, and mints, as well as a variety of scented geraniums.

Where: Well-Sweep Herb Farm is located at 205 Mount Bethel Road, Port Murray. From I-78, take State 31 north to Washington. At the light in Washington, make a right onto State 57 east. Follow State 57 for three miles to the traffic light and make a left onto County 629 north. Continue past the firehouse, make a right onto Rockport Road, and proceed one mile. Make a left onto Mount Bethel Road. The farm is one mile ahead on the left.

Hours: Tuesday through Saturday from 9:30 A.M. to 5:00 P.M. and Monday from 1:00 P.M. to 5:00 P.M. Closed on holidays. From January 1 through April 1, call first.

Admission: Free. Tours are available for $3.00 per person for groups of 12 or more. Call for reservations.

Best time to visit: The gardens peak in July and August. The best time to buy plants is in mid-May.

Concessions: A gift shop carries a wide variety of items, including books, potpourri supplies, baskets, candles, and pottery, as well as dried flowers that the Hydes grow in their fields.

Other: Courses are offered year-round. Call for a free newsletter. A catalog of everything sold at the farm costs $2.00.
For more information: Well-Sweep Herb Farm, 205 Mount Bethel Road, Port Murray, NJ 07865. Call 908-852-5390.

Leonard J. Buck Garden

When Leonard J. Buck decided to develop the 33-acre, wooded stream valley of his estate, he collaborated with the well-known rock garden designer Zenon Schreiber. His goal was to create a naturalistic garden that would incorporate several large rock outcroppings existing on the property. The result was the creation of one of the premier rock gardens in the eastern United States.

The Leonard J. Buck Garden in Somerset County provides a unique setting of woods, streams, and rock outcroppings. There are extensive collections of rhododendrons, dogwoods, and other woodland plants, including wildflowers, ferns, and alpines, all thriving in an ecologically correct habitat that appears far from being man-made.

We were greeted upon our arrival to the garden with the sight of a caramel-colored cat lazily stretching in the sunshine in the courtyard of the visitors center, the estate's renovated carriage house. The cat summed up the atmosphere of the garden, where the lush stands of trees and scenic trails offer the perfect place to relax and unwind.

Several brochures available at the visitors center will greatly enhance your trip through the garden by helping to explain and point out many of the garden's highlights, including the supporting rock scenery, the raised peninsula bed of heaths and heathers, and the wide variety of ferns.

One of the first things you see when you begin your exploration of the garden is the impressive Big Rock, a flat-topped prominence that rises 20 feet above the garden's meadow and pond. Big Rock is a rock bench, or a remnant of an ancient, valley-wide waterfall. Its flat tip drops off abruptly at a steep rock face, which was exposed and sharpened when the garden was being developed.

Other prehistoric rock outcrops throughout the garden, such as Reno Rock, Horseshoe Rock, Fern Rock, and Little Rock, create different exposures and microclimates that enable the garden's wide variety of plants to thrive.

Some of the notable trees and displays found in the garden are the large dawn redwoods from China, the royal azaleas, large ostrich ferns, and primroses.

The garden is at its peak in the spring when the rhododendrons and wildflowers bloom; however, the varying microclimates and exposures afforded by the garden's many rock outcroppings provide year-round interest.

The garden was donated to the Somerset County Park Commission by Mrs. Helen Buck in 1976.

Where: The Leonard J. Buck Garden is located on Layton Road in Far Hills. From I-287 north, take Exit 22. From I-287 south, take Exit 22B. Follow U.S. 202 north through Far Hills. At the Far Hills train station, turn right just before the tracks onto Liberty Corner Road, go approximately one mile, and turn right again onto Layton Road.

Hours: The garden is open weekdays from 10:00 A.M. to 5:00 P.M., Saturday from 10:00 A.M. to 5:00 P.M., Sunday from noon to 5:00 P.M. Closed weekends and major holidays December through February.

Admission: $1.00 donation per person is requested.

Best time to visit: Spring.

Activities: Guided tours for groups can be arranged for a fee. Please call for advance reservations.

Concessions: None.

Other: The visitors center houses the Buck Garden offices, a meeting room, and rest rooms. Picnicking and pets are prohibited.

For more information: Somerset County Park Commission, Leonard J. Buck Garden, 11 Layton Road, Far Hills, NJ 07931. Call 908-234-2677.

Pyramid Mountain

Pyramid Mountain has more than 1,000 acres of rugged trails, fields, cliffs, and waterfalls, but the big payoffs for hiking it are the geological oddities you'll find along the way.

Pyramid Mountain is perhaps best known as the site of Tripod Rock, a unique glacial erratic that was deposited by the Wisconsin glacier more than 10,000 years ago and is believed to have been a sacred place for the Lenni-Lenapes. What makes this 240-ton boulder so unusual is that it is precariously balanced on three smaller boulders.

Pyramid Mountain also is known for its wildlife and more than 400 species of native wildflowers and plants. While you're hiking the trails, you can appreciate the beauty of the chestnut oak, mountain laurel, cardinal flower, and other native flora. More than 100 species of birds and 30 species of mammals have been sighted in the area. These include the great blue heron, barred owl, kestrel, Cooper's hawk, osprey, saw-whet, and screech and great horned owls, as well as the bobcat, bear, and beaver.

That Pyramid Mountain is protected today as a natural and recreational park is a tribute to a group of local activists, headed by Lucy Meyer of Kinnelon, who fought to preserve it. (Lucy's Overlook, off the blue trail, is named after her.) At various times, luxury housing has been proposed here. But the Committee to Save Pyramid Mountain worked with state, county, and municipal officials to preserve 725 acres as of 1993, and another 600 surrounding acres are close to being preserved. The group's ultimate goal is to preserve 3,500 acres over four adjacent mountain ranges—Pyramid Mountain, Stony Brook Mountain, Turkey Mountain, and Rock Pear.

There are half a dozen hiking trails to choose from when visiting Pyramid Mountain. We chose the blue trail, which features some steep hiking over a boulder-strewn path, but overall is not too difficult. The blue trail connects with the white trail, and it's the white trail that leads to Tripod Rock. We visited on a holiday, and while there were many hikers, it was easy enough to find solitude along the way by resting a few minutes and letting any tailgaters pass us. We weren't eager for any human companionship, but we couldn't resist stopping to pet the many dogs that were happily clambering up the mountain alongside their owners.

We thought Tripod Rock, at an elevation of 806 feet, would be a great place to stop, rest, and have lunch. Of course, if we thought that, so did everyone else. If you visit on a weekend or holiday, don't expect to be able to soak up one of nature's wonders all by yourself, at least not for too long. And if you don't want to be included in everyone else's pictures, don't park yourself right next to the rock while you eat lunch. (If you're the family of four who visited on Labor Day, give us a call. We have some great shots of you eating.)

Some people believe that two smaller perched boulders near Tripod Rock were used as an ancient calendar by early inhabitants. On the summer solstice, or the longest day of the year, the sunset is visible between these boulders. It is believed that the sun would set directly above a sighting rock on Stony Brook Mountain. Although a boulder was found in the approximate area of Stony Brook, it had been bulldozed from its original location. Therefore, no one will ever really know for sure whether this site was used to determine when it was time, for example, for the early inhabitants to begin collecting medicinal herbs and other useful plants.

If you choose the white/blue trail on your return trip, you'll get to see Bear Rock, which is at least 10 times the size of Tripod and is one of the largest glacial erratics in the state. Follow the white trail from here back to the parking lot. Our entire trip took less than three hours.

Where: Pyramid Mountain is located within Kinnelon Borough and Montville Township, Morris County. From I-287, exit at Main Street, Boonton. Turn right onto Boonton Avenue (County 511) and follow it to the end. Make a right, then an immediate left. The visitors center and parking lot are eight-tenths of a mile on the left.
Hours: Trails are open daily from 8:00 A.M. to dusk. The visitors center is open Friday through Sunday from 10:00 A.M. to 4:30 P.M.
Admission: Free.
Best time to visit: Year-round.
Activities: Hiking, bird-watching, and observing botany and geology are popular activities.
Concessions: None.
Pets: Allowed on a six-foot leash.
Other: Rest rooms, exhibits, and trail guides can be found in the visitors center.
For more information: Pyramid Mountain Visitors Center, 472A Boonton Avenue, Boonton, NJ 07005. Call 973-334-3130.

Great Swamp National Wildlife Refuge

There was something about the still and virtually untouched landscape of this unique wilderness that made us tread lightly and lower our voices as soon as we stepped into it.

The Great Swamp National Wildlife Refuge contains approximately 7,450 acres of diverse habitat, including hardwood swamp, upland timber, marshes, streams, ponds, and poorly drained pasture, which support a wide variety of wildlife and attract more than 300,000 visitors a year. A wildlife observation area, as well as nearly eight miles of trails, give you ample opportunity to explore this protected area.

Great Swamp is descended from Glacial Lake Passaic, which existed thousands of years ago. The huge lake was formed as the Wisconsin glacier withdrew northward, leaving behind sand and gravel that blocked the outlet of an ancient river basin. Melting water from the glacier flowed into the basin to form the giant lake.

Eventually, the retreating glacier uncovered a second outlet at what is now Little Falls Gap, and the lake waters drained out along the Passaic River. The lake disappeared and was replaced by extensive marshes and swamps, one of which was Great Swamp.

In 1708, the Delaware Indians deeded to English investors a 30,000-acre tract, including what is now known as Great Swamp. Later, settlements sprang up in the area, and during the Revolutionary War, local settlers fashioned wagon wheel parts with wood cut from the Great Swamp. By 1844, farms appeared on cleared uplands, but small farming operations eventually became uneconomical and gradually disappeared. As a result, the cleared upland returned to woods and the lower flat areas reverted to swampland.

Various modern uses for Great Swamp were talked about over the years, but it was a proposal in 1959 to site a jet airport here that sparked a preservation movement. Through the efforts of the Great Swamp Committee of the North American Wildlife Foundation and many volunteers, more than a million dollars was raised to purchase nearly 3,000 acres, which were donated to the U.S. Department of the Interior. Through the years, additional acres have been added to the original tract.

When visiting the refuge, the best place to start is at the refuge office, where you can pick up a map. Next, head out to the wildlife observation center off Long Hill Road, which is an especially good place if you are interested in wildlife-spotting or photography.

The center features approximately one mile of trails, interpretive displays, an unstaffed information booth, and blinds for observing a variety of birds. Depending on the time of year, you might see great blue herons, mallards, wood ducks, and hawks here. The boardwalk that travels past the rest rooms crosses a marshy area where frogs and reptiles, such as painted and snapping turtles, often can be seen.

The wildlife observation center is situated in the wildlife management area in the western half of the refuge. Here, water levels are regulated; grasslands and brush are mowed periodically to maintain habitat and species diversity; nesting structures for wood ducks, bluebirds, and other birds are provided; and research studies are conducted.

The eastern half of the refuge has been designated by Congress as a wilderness area. Here, hiking is permitted on almost eight miles of trails. Use of this sensitive area is limited to foot travel to preserve the wilderness experience. The trails often are very wet, so waterproof footgear or old sneakers are recommended.

The refuge features many large old oak and beech trees, stands of mountain laurel, and several hundred species of trees, shrubs, aquatic plants, ferns, sedges, grasses, and other forms of plant life. It also is home to many animals; in the morning and toward evening, visitors are likely to see wild turkey and white-tailed deer in and near the fields. The red fox and raccoon are common, but rarely seen during daylight hours. Muskrats are frequently seen in wet areas at dawn and dusk, especially during the spring. Various kinds of fish, reptiles, and amphibians also are found here, including the blue-spotted salamander and the bog turtle, which are endangered in New Jersey.

The refuge was established to provide migration, nesting, and feeding habitats for migratory birds, and a total of 223 species of birds have been identified to date here. The best season to see waterfowl and other marsh and water birds is during their early spring migrations, before marsh vegetation emerges to hide them. May is the best time to see warblers and other songbirds. The threatened bald eagle, the barn owl, and the pileated woodpecker are among the species that occasionally have been spotted.

The best times for observing wildlife are early morning and late afternoon. When there are many people around, such as on Sunday afternoon, your chances of spotting wildlife decrease dramatically. From May to September, you should use insect repellent and wear protective clothing to discourage mosquitoes, ticks, and deerflies.

Environmental centers are located on either side of the refuge. The Somerset County Park Commission's Environmental Education Center at Lord Stirling Park, located in Basking Ridge on the western border of the refuge, offers a varied program of environmental education courses, guided field trips, and 8.5 miles of walking trails. For more information, call 908-766-2489. The Great Swamp Outdoor Education Center is run by the Morris County Park Commission and is located on the eastern side of the refuge off Southern Boulevard in Chatham. This center also offers a varied natural science program of classes and guided tours and provides one mile of trail and boardwalk for the public. For more information, call 973-635-6629.

Where: Great Swamp is located seven miles south of Morristown. From I-78, take Exit 40 in Gillette. Turn onto Hillcrest

Road (it's a right turn from I-78 west, a left turn from I-78 east). Hillcrest becomes Mountain Avenue, then Meyersville Road. Proceed until you come to a small circle in the center of Meyersville. Follow signs to refuge office. From I-287, exit at North Maple Avenue. Stay on North Maple, turning left at the second "Great Swamp" sign onto Lord Stirling Road. Follow signs to refuge office.

Hours: Trail use at the wildlife refuge is permitted during daylight hours. The refuge office is open weekdays from 8:00 A.M. to 4:30 P.M. During spring and fall, it also may be open on Sunday. Call ahead for information.

Admission: Free.

Best time to visit: Spring and fall for bird-watching.

Activities: Hiking, photography, and wildlife watching are popular.

Concessions: The Somerset County Park Commission's Environmental Education Center sells books and gifts related to the environment.

Pets: Must be leashed and remain in parking areas.

Other: Vehicles may be parked only in designated areas. Picnicking and camping are not permitted. Groups of 10 to 15 people can schedule a guided tour. Movies and slide talks can be scheduled for groups of up to 50. Lists of birds, mammals, wildflowers, and reptiles and amphibians, as well as a refuge map, are available at the refuge office.

For more information: Great Swamp National Wildlife Refuge, 152 Pleasant Plains Road, Basking Ridge, NJ 07920. Call 973-425-1222.

2

Delaware Water Gap

There is no greater place in New Jersey to view the power and splendor of nature than at the Delaware Water Gap. Millions of years ago, the forces of nature uplifted this once-level plain and formed the ridges and lush valleys of the gap today.

The gap is noted as being one of the most interesting geological formations in the eastern United States. Both the Kittatinny Ridge of the Appalachian Mountains and the nearby Pennsylvania hills framing the valley are carved with countless mountain streams, waterfalls, glacial lakes, gorges, and other natural attractions.

From millions of years of change among the plateaus, mountains, and valleys emerged the Delaware River. It cut its way through the sandstone and rock of the Kittatinny Ridge and formed the famous Delaware Water Gap as it made its way to the ocean. Amazingly, the Delaware River travels nearly the same course today that it did millions of years ago.

The Delaware River always has attracted people to this scenic area. Early settlers were drawn by the wildlife, fertile soil, and endless freshwater supply. The "Lumbermen of the Delaware," as they were called by locals, also were drawn to the area where the river provided an efficient shipping route for timber gathered from the surrounding woodlands. The original inhabitants along the river were the Minsi, a branch of the Lenni-Lenape Indians. The geographic region of the Upper Delaware River Valley that reaches for 40 miles on both sides of the river derives its name, Minisink, from these early inhabitants.

Many meanings of the name Minisink have been offered, but the best known is "where the waters have gone," spoken by an observant Indian who noted that the entire fertile area had once been covered by a vast body of water before the Indians' time. The earliest known Paleo-Indian occupation of the Minisink is believed to be 8640 B.C.

Dozens of sites along the banks of the Delaware River in the Minisink offer substantial proof of occupation by thousands of Native Americans at various times.

Dutch explorer Henry Hudson "discovered" the Delaware River in 1609. Early European settlers in search of freedom and independence named the river after Lord De La Warr, the governor of the English colony at Jamestown, Virginia, in 1610.

During the mid-1800s and early 1900s, large resorts and hotels were constructed amid the hills surrounding the Delaware Water Gap, and the major purpose of the river changed from transportation to recreation.

Today, the Delaware Water Gap National Recreation Area and such surrounding areas as New Jersey's Worthington State Forest offer visitors the perfect setting for picnicking, canoeing, hiking, camping, rock climbing, hunting, and many other outdoor activities.

The Delaware Water Gap National Recreation Area was set aside by Congress in 1965 to preserve 70,000 acres of land for public use. In 1978, 40 miles of the Delaware River also were designated a Wild and Scenic River by Congress, meaning the river is undammed and its streams, shoreline, and adjacent land are maintained in their natural states.

The Delaware Water Gap National Recreation Area offers more than 60 miles of hiking trails. A guide containing some of the more popular and accessible trails throughout the region is available at the Kittatinny Point Visitors Center, located between I-80 and the river at the last exit before the toll bridge. You also can pick up recommended topographical maps for backcountry hiking here.

Fishing is also popular at the gap. Muskellunge, pike, bass, perch, walleye, bluegill, catfish, and trout are all likely catches during a day's outing. As spring approaches and water temperatures rise, the American shad starts its spawning journey from the Atlantic coastline and heads up toward the Delaware. In the Delaware, shad fishing has become a popular annual event.

To fully appreciate the Delaware River, we recommend a canoe trip down it. Access points are located every eight to ten miles along the river, allowing for easy day trips. You'll be able to experience and enjoy the river in much the same way as the Lenni-Lenape Indians did, who once could be seen traveling in chestnut-log canoes along the river.

Canoe camping is allowed under special conditions. It is strictly limited to canoeists traveling from one access point to another, when the distance between those points is too great to be covered in one day. Camping is permitted at those sites posted with the National Park System's camping sign. Maps and additional information about camping, canoeing, and other park activities are available at the Kittatinny Point Visitors Center. A special river guide is also sold at the center.

Take special heed of the rules and regulations of the National Park Service while canoeing or boating the river. The Delaware has strong currents, sharp drop-offs, and constantly changing conditions. Wear a life jacket, bring an adequate water supply, and never swim alone. For more information, contact any park ranger or call the National Recreation Area's 24-hour number: 717-588-2435. In an emergency, call 800-543-4295.

The Kittatinny Point Visitors Center is open daily from 9:00 A.M. to 5:00 P.M. from April through October. October through March it's open on weekends from 9:00 A.M. to 4:30 P.M. For more information, call the Kittatinny Point Visitors Center at 908-496-4458.

Worthington State Forest

Just north of the Delaware Water Gap in Warren County is one of New Jersey's most rustic and scenic recreation areas, Worthington State Forest. The forest extends six miles along the crest of the Kittatinny Ridge, where, except for fields along the Delaware River, it is completely covered in lush woodland.

We arrived at the park office early on a Friday morning and were lucky enough to have our pick of campsites along the river. The ranger recommended several sites, and after a quick tour of the area we chose one of the most remote and incredibly scenic spots we'd come across in our travels through the state.

We set up our tent on a raised bank facing the river's clear running waters. From the thick canopy of trees above, acorns dropped into the cushioned silence of the woods. At the break of dawn, we were greeted with the crisp mountain air and the peaceful sight of early morning fog rising from the river.

We had found our own wooded haven away from the rush of the metropolitan area, and we savored every minute of it. Our only visitors during our three-day stay were a family of three deer, a brave skunk ambling in for dinner, and rain, which made our last night's stay a little damp, but no less enjoyable.

Worthington State Forest contains 5,830 acres of some of the most rugged terrain found in northern New Jersey. Elevations above sea level range from 300 feet at the river's edge to 1,480 feet at the top of the ridge at the northern boundary. The river valley is rich in Native American lore, and visitors have found arrowheads and pieces of old pottery. When in bloom, mountain laurel, rhododendron, witch hazel, and dogwood add rich color to the encompassing dense woodlands.

The first trade highway in the country, the Old Mine Road, passes through the forest along the river. The road was built by early Dutch settlers to transport heavy mining loads from Pahaquarry Township, Warren County, northward through Sussex County to New York, where the ore was then shipped to Holland.

It's ironic that, after completing the Old Mine Road, a major engineering feat for those times, settlers made very little profit from their mining endeavors in the region. However, early settlers did use the road regularly to transport wheat and cider to nearby areas where they traded for other goods. Several historic Dutch farms still stand alongside the road, affording visitors the chance to witness some of the area's rich history.

Miles of old wooded roads along the mountain are perfect for day hiking. Part of the Appalachian Trail also crosses the river from Pennsylvania just above the Delaware Water Gap, ascends the mountain ridge, and continues through the forest to its upper boundary.

Bird-watchers as well as hikers will enjoy the many scenic trails. A variety of bird species can be seen throughout the forest, including some common nesting ones, such as ruffed grouse, broad-winged hawks, wild turkeys, barred owls, cuckoos, woodcocks, and eastern screeches. Some less common species that may be seen are the endangered Cooper's hawk, the threatened northern goshawk, the purple finch, and the whippoorwill.

Worthington State Forest supports one of the most prolific deer herds in New Jersey, thanks to the land's previous owner and namesake, Charles C. Worthington. He originally used his property as a wildlife hunting preserve and reintroduced the white-tailed deer to the area. The state acquired the land in 1954.

There are several points of interest that you shouldn't miss while visiting Worthington State Forest, including the Dunnfield Creek and Sunfish Pond Natural Areas and the steep, scenic summit of Mount Tammany. Each of the areas can be reached from trails from within the park or from parking lots along I-80.

Sunfish Pond Natural Area

Sunfish Pond was known to the Native Americans as "hidden lake," an appropriate description for this rare, spring-fed lake situated high in the folds of the Kittatinny Mountains. From the nearest point along the Delaware River, it is at least a 2.5-mile hike to its remote banks and crystal waters.

The 41-acre Sunfish Pond, designated as a National Landmark in 1970, is the last remaining glacial lake in New Jersey. A trail follows along the lake's mile-and-a-half perimeter.

Preservation of the unspoiled, natural pond was a victory for local conservationists, who led the effort to save the land, which once was targeted by utility companies for use as a pumped-storage reservoir for generating electrical power.

With a variety of trails to choose from, we decided to take the Appalachian Trail, a 3.75-mile hike starting from the parking lot located just off I-80. You can also reach Sunfish Pond from Old Mine Road by the Worthington State Forest camping grounds via a shorter trail of less than three miles.

The Appalachian Trail parallels Dunnfield Creek for a distance through a lush hemlock forest. Dunnfield Creek Natural

Area surrounds the clear, rock-strewn creek falling more than 1,000 feet from Mount Tammany to the Delaware River. The creek is designated a National Wild and Scenic Trout Stream.

The trail eventually veers away from the scenic gorge in a gradual ascent toward the pond. It took us a little more than two hours to make the hike, which is well worth the trip. Not only is the hike up the winding trail of the ridge a pleasant and scenic way to spend the day, but the beautiful mountain lake that awaits you with its crystal clear water and surrounding wilderness setting is a sight you'll not soon forget.

Besides attracting many visitors during the year, the pond also is a migratory stop for waterfowl during the spring and fall. Species likely to be found here during migration include Canada geese, mallard ducks, black ducks, pintails, goldeneyes, scaup, bufflehead, and various mergansers. In addition to migratory waterfowl, many raptors, including threatened ospreys and endangered bald eagles, pass through the area.

White-tailed deer, wild turkeys, ruffed grouse, and gray squirrels are some other species that can be seen in the pond area. Some people suspect that there never has been an abundant or diversified fish population in Sunfish Pond. Because of the chemical and geological composition of the area, it is highly acidic and can host only a few hardy species, including pumpkinseed sunfish, chain pickerel, yellow perch, and brown bullheads.

At one time, because of the pond's location at 1,382 feet above sea level, few people visited the site. However, today the pond is a popular spot for hikers and birders alike. We were determined to find a little solitude away from the small crowd that had gathered, which really wasn't that difficult once we stepped off the beaten path and bushwhacked our way to privacy.

We found our own spot along the pond's surrounding boulders, unpacked our lunches, and enjoyed the tranquillity of one of the last remaining natural lakes in the northern Appalachian Highlands.

Mount Tammany

We were expecting to find ridges too steep to climb and too strenuous to enjoy when we began our hike on the Red Dot Trail to Mount Tammany. But what we found instead was one of the most scenic and dramatic trails located along the rocky terrain of the Kittatinny Range.

We were warned by friends that the "red trail" up to Mount Tammany was rough and steep, and then warned again by the ranger at the Kittatinny Point Visitors Center. The trail is steep, leading about a mile and a half straight up to the summit roughly 1,200 feet above the Delaware. But if you take your time and bring an adequate water supply, you'll be rewarded with an incredible view of the Delaware Water Gap from the top.

Like many areas throughout the Delaware Water Gap region, Mount Tammany's name originates from the Lenni-Lenapes. It was named after the Lenape chief Tamenund. In fact, the entire Kittatinny Range was named by the Indians—Kittatinny means "endless mountains."

The red trail begins at the first parking lot on I-80 west. It gradually ascends along a well-worn path. About halfway up to the summit, you'll come to one of the many impressive overlooks along the trail, which only get better as you climb.

The trail levels off at one point about a half-mile from the start, offering a perfect place to rest and take in your surroundings. You're about a third of the way to the summit at that point. There is one rough ledge along the trail that takes some maneuvering to get over, which may be one of the reasons why the ranger and past hikers of the red trail don't recommend it for young children.

It takes a little more than an hour to reach the summit of Mount Tammany, where a view of the Delaware River Valley framed by Mount Minisi on the Pennsylvania side of the river is extraordinary.

We sat quietly on the ridge for almost an hour, watching the graceful flight patterns of about eight hawks. From our seats upon the scattered rocks of the ledge, we witnessed for ourselves the spectacular geologic phenomenon of the Delaware Water Gap.

Where: Worthington State Forest is easily accessible off I-80 west to the Delaware Water Gap. Take the last New Jersey exit road before crossing the Delaware River toll bridge and continue north along the eastern shore of the river. The forest office is 3.5 miles north of the exit.

Hours: The forest is open for camping from April 1 through December 31. The forest office is open from 8:00 A.M. to 4:30 P.M. year-round.

Admission: Campsites are $10.00 per night with flush toilets and $8.00 per night without flush toilets. Group campsites are also available for a nominal fee.

Best time to visit: Spring, summer, and fall.

Activities: Fishing, swimming, hiking, camping, boating, cross-country skiing, and hunting are permitted. Hunting is permitted on the mountain (you can't shoot across the Appalachian Trail), and fishing is permitted from both the shore and by boat.

Concessions: None.

Other: A ramp for launching small boats is centrally located within the camping area. There is no motor size restriction on the Delaware River, but there are speed limits: 10 mph from April 1 through September 30, and 35 mph from October 1 through March 31. There is one backpacker campsite along the Appalachian Trail. Campsites for family and group camping are provided along two miles of the river frontage. The sites have spaces for tents, tent trailers, or small travel trailers and are equipped with tables and fire pits. Camping, swimming, boating, and fires are prohibited at Sunfish Pond to preserve the pond and its natural surroundings.

For more information: Worthington State Forest, HC 62, Box 2, Columbia, NJ 07832. Call 908-841-9575.

3

Gateway Region

The New Jersey State Botanical Garden at Ringwood State Park

Nestled in the valley of the Ramapo Mountains in northern Passaic County is Skylands Manor, once the home of Clarence McKenzie Lewis, an investment banker and trustee of the New York Botanical Garden. His intention upon purchasing the property was to create a botanical showplace. The result was the great classic garden known today as the official New Jersey State Botanical Garden.

Located in Ringwood State Park, the manor and its grounds provide the opportunity to see more than 5,000 species, varieties, and horticultural forms. For 30 years, Lewis collected plants from all over the world and hired the most prominent landscape architects of his day from the firm Vitale and Geiffert. With the help of more than 60 gardeners in peak seasons, Lewis maintained one of the finest collections of plants in the state.

Skylands Manor House and Gardens were purchased in 1966 by the state of New Jersey from Shelton College, which had used the 1,117-acre tract of land as a campus. The gardens surrounding the manor make up the only botanical garden in the state park system. A rambling Tudor mansion built with

49

native granite, the manor is a historically accurate reproduction of an English Jacobean house.

It is impossible to ignore the historical significance of the land as you walk along the gardens surrounding Skylands Manor, where none of the layouts of the formal gardens have been changed from the original designs. Lewis stressed symmetry, color, texture, form, and fragrance in his gardens, attributes that still appeal to the garden's visitors today.

There are several attractions at the gardens, including the Crab Apple Vista, the Winter Garden, and the Azalea Garden. The Crab Apple Vista blooms in early May, when a profusion of pink blossoms stretches a half-mile up a gentle slope to the manor's lodge. The Winter Garden features New Jersey's largest Jeffrey pine, as well as a Japanese umbrella pine noted for its bold dark green needles and densely conical appearance. Other interesting trees include a 70-foot, glossy-needled Algerian fir grown from seed in 1931 and the graceful Atlas cedar, also a native of North Africa.

The Azalea Garden is located in a particularly scenic spot, where banks of azaleas and rhododendrons border a reflecting pool. Lily pads in an array of striking colors from hot pink to yellow bloom in the pool, a perfect subject for photographs.

Other garden displays include the Annual Garden, Perennial Border, Lilac Garden, Peony Garden, Summer Garden, Magnolia Walk, and the Octagonal Garden.

Although the brilliant botanical gardens of Skylands Manor are the main attractions at Ringwood State Park, there are many other worthwhile features and activities.

The Ringwood Manor House is a National Historic Landmark located within the park. The manor stands as a reminder of the area's iron industry, which started at Ringwood in 1740 with the formation of the Ringwood Company. In the mid-1800s, the property was purchased by Abram S. Hewitt, America's foremost ironmaster. In 1936, the Ringwood Manor

House and its surrounding 95 acres were deeded to the state of New Jersey by Erskine Hewitt, who wished to preserve the historic property for posterity.

The Ringwood River is popular with anglers who visit the park. The river is stocked annually with rainbow and brown trout. Trout, largemouth bass, sunfish, pickerel, and catfish can be found in Shepherd Lake, where the spring-fed waters also provide a refreshing bathing area. Hiking is popular along the park's marked trails, where you can explore the surrounding woodlands and experience the excellent views from the park's high elevations.

You also can picnic along the Ringwood River and Shepherd Lake. Tables and grills are provided for both family and group picnic sites.

Where: Ringwood State Park can be reached by State 23 and County 511 from the west and State 17 and Sloatsburg Road from the east.

Hours: The park is open daily from sunrise to sunset year-round. The park office is open daily from 8:00 A.M. to 4:30 P.M. year-round.

Admission: $2.00 parking fee from Memorial Day weekend through Labor Day weekend for Ringwood Manor.

Best time to visit: Year-round.

Activities: Boating, picnicking, hunting, fishing, bathing, hiking, cross-country skiing, and snowmobiling are permitted. Tours also are offered of the park's two historic houses. Call for more information.

Concessions: Rowboats, canoes, and small sailboats can be rented at the boathouse concession on Shepherd Lake. A concession for trap and skeet shooting also is available at Shepherd Lake.

Other: There are no camping facilities at the park.
For more information: Ringwood State Park, P.O. Box 1304, Ringwood, NJ 07456. Call 973-962-7031.

Reeves-Reed Arboretum

The sounds of chamber music greeted us as we walked from the parking lot toward the Reeves-Reed Arboretum and the nearby education center. The music was the perfect added touch to the serene wooded scene, but not exactly a standard extra. We were curious, and as we approached we discovered the music's source. A group of musicians was providing the perfect background for a garden wedding ceremony.

We even bumped into the bride when we entered the main building, a beautiful Colonial Revival residence that serves as the garden's administrative office and houses all of the garden's handy trail guides and brochures. Needless to say, we looked a little out of place with our hiking boots and notebooks, but we managed to sneak away without attracting too much attention.

The Reeves-Reed Arboretum is a nonprofit educational conservancy focusing on trees, shrubs, flora, and herbaceous plants. The more than 12 acres of hardwood forest, open fields, lawns, and formal gardens are preserved for study and public enjoyment. The arboretum is a National and State Historic Site, and its gardens and house are newly restored.

Although small compared to many of the arboretums throughout the state, Reeves-Reed Arboretum has plenty to offer. It not only has interesting geologic features and distinct habitats—low, wetland woods and dry, upland areas—but it also is one of the few arboretums that provides such a wide variety of educational lectures, workshops, and field trips.

More than 1,500 schoolchildren from local counties enroll each year in "Networks to Nature" classes. The arboretum provides the perfect natural setting for children to explore rocks, minerals, plants, trees, and other natural vegetation and topography.

One of the interesting geologic characteristics of the surrounding acreage is the kettles, or depressions, formed as the Wisconsin glacier retreated more than 10,000 years ago. A large kettle, situated near the front of the house and often referred to as the "bowl," is a natural showcase of April daffodils and summer field flowers.

Guides to the arboretum's woodland trails, rose garden, and herb garden are available at the main house. There are also guides to the area's wildlife habitat and a bloom guide to help visitors learn the peak seasons of the local flora. The azalea garden, located on the side of the main house, is an especially scenic area in the spring; that's where we unwittingly crashed the garden wedding ceremony.

In 1974, local citizens financed the purchase of this former country estate as an arboretum in cooperation with the city of Summit. The estate dates back to 1889 when John Hornor Wisner built his family home, today known as the Wisner House. He hired New York landscape architect Calvert Vaux, who, with partner Frederick Law Olmsted, designed Central Park. In 1993, the Reeves-Reed estate was designated as both a National and State Historic Site.

In 1916, the property was sold to Mr. and Mrs. Richard Reeves, who commissioned top New York landscape designers, including Ellen Shipman, to plan the formal gardens. When the Charles L. Reed family acquired the estate in 1968, they added the woodland trails and the herb garden. While visiting the arboretum, take special notice of the herb garden's design. The herb garden is laid out in an interesting pattern of concentric circles within a square, an ancient pattern believed to bring good luck and fortune.

The newly enlarged Garden Shop on the premises features fine botanical porcelains, whimsical and classic selections of garden sculptures, and a generous supply of gardening tools and equipment.

Where: The Reeves-Reed Arboretum is located in Summit just off of State 24, at the Hobart exit, via State 124 to Hobart Avenue.

Hours: The grounds are open daily from sunrise to sunset year-round. The office, in the Wisner House, is open weekdays from 9:00 A.M. to 3:00 P.M. A botanical/horticultural library is open for browsing during office hours. The Garden Shop is open Monday through Saturday from 10:00 A.M. to 4:00 P.M.

Admission: Free.

Best time to visit: Year-round.

Activities: In addition to the special lectures, workshops, and field trips relating to home gardening, horticulture, landscape design, plant identification, and environmental issues, the arboretum also periodically features a free "Sunday Afternoon Series" of concerts and lectures. Call for more information.

Concessions: None.

Other: Rest rooms and the education center are located inside the main house. Both are wheelchair-accessible.

For more information: Reeves-Reed Arboretum, 165 Hobart Avenue, Summit, NJ 07901. Call 908-273-8787. The Garden Shop, 908-277-1190.

Great Falls of the Passaic River

It might seem a bit strange to go looking for one of New Jersey's natural wonders right in the middle of the state's third largest city, but it was the powerful Great Falls of the Passaic River that inspired the birth of Paterson, the nation's first planned industrial city.

Great Falls of the Passaic River

It was in the late 1700s that Alexander Hamilton, an advocate of industrialization for the new country, first glimpsed the 77-foot falls and realized the potential of harnessing the energy from the Passaic River. Pierre Charles L'Enfant, who designed Washington, D.C., came up with the idea for a system of elevated raceways that would carry water to the mills of Paterson and enable them to use this power. His idea was modified by Peter Colt of Connecticut, who designed a simpler and more economical raceway system.

Paterson's industries produced everything from linen and silk to aircraft engines and steam locomotives over the next two centuries. By the end of the 19th century, in fact, the presence of 300 silk mills earned the city the title "Silk City of the World."

Today, you can see Paterson's beginnings by taking a tour of the Great Falls Historic District. Here, you can stop in the visitors center and pick up a copy of the self-guided walking tour that starts at the falls. As you leave the visitors center, walk the short distance to Great Falls Park. While crossing the second of two footbridges, you'll get a breathtaking view of rushing water cascading over a 280-foot-wide chasm. At peak times, up to 165,000 gallons of water per second flow over the falls.

Also along the tour, you'll see the Paterson Museum, which originally was an assembly plant for locomotives and now houses artifacts from the city's industrial beginnings, former mills that have been converted into schools, art galleries and shops, and housing, as well as remnants of the raceway system.

Where: The Paterson Historic District is accessible from I-80, the Garden State Parkway, and State 4.

Hours: The visitors center is open weekdays from 9:00 A.M. to 4:00 P.M. and on weekends and holidays by appointment. From May 1 through October 30, the center is also open on weekends from noon to 4:00 P.M. The Paterson Museum is open Tuesday through Friday from 10:00 A.M. to 4:00 P.M. and on weekends from 12:30 P.M. to 4:30 P.M. It is closed on national holidays.

Admission: The self-guided tour is free. The Paterson Museum appreciates a $2.00 donation per adult.

Best time to visit: An ideal time to visit the falls is 24 to 48 hours after a heavy storm, when the additional water heightens the thunderous effect.

Concessions: Shops are located within the historic district.

Pets: Dogs are permitted, but must be on a leash and strictly controlled.

Other: Guided tours are offered as a service for groups of at least 10 people by appointment only. There is no charge for guided tours, but donations are appreciated. Self-guiding tour maps and other information are available at the visitors center or by mail. The city sponsors an annual Great Falls Festival over Labor Day weekend.

For more information: Great Falls Visitor Center, 65 McBride Avenue Extension, Great Falls Historic District, Paterson, NJ 07501-1715. Call 973-279-9587.

Flat Rock Brook Nature Center

It was in the heart of the fall season when we meandered our way along the trails of the Flat Rock Brook Nature Center. A long golden carpet of sweet gum and tulip leaves covered almost the entire 3.2 miles of trail, which led us through one of the last stands of forest along the primeval Palisades in Englewood.

Situated on the western slope of the Palisades cliffs, only four miles from New York City, the trails of Flat Rock Brook Nature Center offer visitors a rare opportunity to explore a range of geological features, from volcanic bedrock formations, quarry cliffs, and a cascading stream to ponds, meadows, and wetlands.

The cliffs, which stretch from Staten Island about 50 miles northwest to Haverstraw, New York, formed about 190 million years ago when hot molten rock was squeezed horizontally between layers of sandstone and shale. Sandwiched between these sedimentary rocks, the magma cooled and solidified into the igneous material known as diabase.

The center was established in 1973 by a group of local citizens dedicated to land conservation and environmental education. Today, the 150 acres of native woodlands provide a perfect setting for hiking, bird-watching, and natural history observation in northern New Jersey. The center sponsors environmental programs, after-school classes, and tours for all age groups.

The center and nature preserve were named after the last remaining unchanneled natural waterway of significant size in the Englewood area, which was one of the original reasons why the land was sought for preservation. Today, the center's primary purpose is to maintain a sanctuary for plant and animal life and provide a place for all to enjoy and learn more about the environment.

We began our hike on the white trail, which is located right outside the back entrance of the center, where a pond—bordered by a beautiful weeping willow and an array of colorful native trees and shrubs—was currently the playground for seven mallards. The center's naturalist said there also had been recent sightings in the pond area of two green herons, a solitary sandpiper, a kingfisher, and a great blue heron.

An extensive network of self-guiding trails leads you through many similar, scenic sites throughout the wooded area, where you might also catch a glimpse of chipmunks, frogs, raccoons, butterflies, foxes, and an occasional deer.

The 900-foot Quarry Boardwalk, located in the front of the center, allows access to the surrounding area for the disabled, senior citizens, and small children, so they also can experience the beauty of the area. The trail winds through woods, around a wildflower meadow, and beneath quarry cliffs, ending on a small dock overlooking the pond.

A central focus for the nature preserve is the Flat Rock Brook Nature Center, a beautiful brown clapboard building with large picture windows. The rooms include a staff office, a meeting room, a children's workroom, a library, and a greenhouse/sunroom addition.

A picnic area, located nearby on Jones Road, is a perfect place to bring a bag lunch and enjoy the surroundings. Picnic tables, grills, benches, rest rooms, a playground, and swings are located within the park.

Where: Flat Rock Brook is located in the city of Englewood off State 4, just four miles from New York City. It is easily accessible from Exit 71 off of I-95.

Hours: The center's office is open weekdays from 9:00 A.M. to 5:00 P.M. Call for weekend hours. The picnic area and trails are open daily from sunrise to sunset year-round.

Admission: Free. There is a fee for most programs.

Best time to visit: Spring and fall.

Activities: Each year in early December the center presents a holiday sale. During the spring, the center features Nature Day, an environmental festival involving environmental groups and featuring nature walks, canoe rides, music, arts and crafts for children, and refreshments. The center can be rented for special events, such as birthday parties, weddings, reunions, anniversaries, and office meetings.

Concessions: None.

Pets: All pets must be leashed.

Other: Trail maps are available at the center.

For more information: Flat Rock Brook Nature Center, 443 Van Nostrand Avenue, Englewood, NJ 07631. Call 201-567-1265.

Liberty Science Center

You can explore the depths of a living salt marsh, peer through a solar telescope, and explore the human brain through a 3-D laser journey all in a day's visit to Liberty Science Center, New Jersey's state-of-the-art science playground. With constant programs, films, exhibits, and demonstrations, the museum is a flurry of activity that's perfect for children on a rainy day.

This nonprofit institution features three themes—environment, health, and invention—each on a different floor and with displays designed to dazzle as well as educate its visitors. On the environment floor, it's not surprising to see a member of the staff walking around carrying a live insect for visitors to see and feel, or children peering through microscopes, digging through trays of soil, and touching dinosaur bones.

But the displays aren't just for children. Simple, hands-on activities are set up to help visitors of all ages. We were impressed. The center fosters a spirit of exploration and self-discovery that carries an important educational message, along with hours of fun.

The center houses the Kodak Omni Theater, which features an eight-story curved screen that surrounds you with images that make you feel like part of the action. You can take a ride in a helicopter cockpit on a racing journey through icy Arctic valleys or between glacial peaks. You might stand inside an erupting volcano, visit a rain forest, swim by a barrier reef, or climb Mount Everest.

Each floor of the museum features a discovery room, where members of the staff direct various exploratory programs. These are interactive areas that feature activities and materials that often are too complex or fragile to put on display.

The Environment Discovery Room, or the Green House, is a place where children can watch the behavior of insects and amphibians, such as woodland ants, lizards, and cockroaches, which are placed for close-up viewing on small tables in aquariums. Paper, crayons, and resource books are provided at every exhibit so that children can write down and draw the different things they see.

A field station also is located on the environment floor, where children can identify seashells, observe a live starfish, and examine plankton under a microscope.

The scientists and engineers who built this world-class education center in 1992 also found a way to let you see the state's insect, the honeybee, hard at work.

Located on one of the outer walls on the environment floor is a cross-section of a honeybee hive. Hundreds of bees constantly fly back and forth through a clear tube connected with the outside of the building. The bees went about their business undisturbed while we stood watching them weave in and out through the intricate patterns of their nest.

You can come nose to nose with a puffer fish in the 60-foot-long viewing tank of the Estuary Exhibit. The tank is filled with living plant and animal species native to the nearby Hudson River ecosystem.

In the Bug Zoo, you'll see such live insects as gigantic Madagascar cockroaches; rare, red-kneed Mexican spiders; and African scorpions. Just around the corner at the Atmosphere Exhibit, you can view sunspots and solar flares from the center's solar telescope mounted in a 20-foot, floor-to-ceiling lighthouse. If you step outside to the outdoor deck of the Atmosphere Exhibit, you also can use a weather station's rain gauge, wind vane, and barometer to forecast the weather.

Throughout the center's four-story atrium, more than 250 of these state-of-the-art interactive exhibits are taking place, creating a fast-paced and fun learning atmosphere that delivers a constant flow of educational messages. Besides learning about the natural world, on other floors you can explore the challenges of invention and the physical sciences, as well as learn about the human body. With support from local technology companies, the center is a pioneer in Distance Learning programs, which are interactive, two-way video seminars and professional development workshops for students and teachers.

Where: The Liberty Science Center is located in Liberty State Park and is easily accessible from Exit 14B of the New Jersey Turnpike. A ferry service is also available from Manhattan. Call 800-53-FERRY. Free bus service is available from the Colgate Ferry and Grove Sheet PATH Station every half hour between 7:30 A.M. and 6:30 P.M.

Hours: The exhibits are open weekdays from 9:30 A.M. to 5:30 P.M. The center is closed on Monday except for the following holidays: Martin Luther King, Jr.'s, birthday, Presidents' Day, Memorial Day, Independence Day, Labor Day, Columbus Day, and the Monday following Christmas.

Admission: $9.50 for adults for the exhibit only, $7.00 for the Kodak Omni Theater, or $13.50 for a combined ticket; $8.50 for students and seniors for the exhibit only, $6.00 for the theater, or $11.50 for a combined ticket; $6.50 for children from ages five to twelve for the exhibit only, $5.00 for the theater, or $9.50 for a combined ticket. All children under twelve must be accompanied by an adult. Individual and corporate special memberships provide free admission to exhibit areas and significant discounts for other center services. Call for information about advance reservations or group rates. There is also a $5.00 parking fee.

Best time to visit: Summer is the peak season. To avoid crowds, try to visit at other times of the year.

Activities: Call for information about daily demonstrations, films showing in the Kodak Omni Theater, or specially planned activities.

Concessions: Laser Lights Café offers buffet-style meals or table service with a panoramic view of the New York skyline. The gift shop, Tools and Toys, features an array of science products, books, and toys that complement the center's events and exhibits.

Other: Schools can schedule field trips at the center. Teachers are encouraged to make advance reservations and visit the center prior to the field trip. This advance visit is free of charge with presentation of school ID.

For more information: Liberty Science Center, Liberty State Park, 251 Phillip Street, Jersey City, NJ 07305-4699. Call 201-200-1000.

The Hackensack Meadowlands Development Commission's Environment Center

Walking the trails of a six-acre landfill and visiting a garbage museum sounds about as far away from the natural world as you can get. To be honest, we weren't exactly excited about our journey to the landfill until a friend of ours, an elementary schoolteacher, said it was a great place to learn about the environment. She was right.

The trail that we hiked is situated along the six-acre Kingsland Overlook where an old landfill has been transformed into a unique landscape of plant and floral communities. Not only is the hike over the old landfill educational, but the trail overlook provides an incredible view of the surrounding acres of tidal-flowed lands, woodlands, marshes, and meadows.

The landfill is one of the "recycling" or restoration projects administered by the Hackensack Meadowlands Development Commission in an effort to save the unique salt marsh area known as the Meadowlands, located in northeastern New Jersey.

The garbage museum is part of the Development Commission's environment center located within the surrounding 1,400-acre wildlife preserve. The center also contains classrooms, an auditorium, and a monitoring laboratory equipped to test marine and botanical life.

In 1969, the state of New Jersey enacted the Hackensack Meadowlands Reclamation and Development Act to preserve and reclaim an area of 32 square miles of the unique meadows. At one time, 50,000 tons of garbage a week, from six counties, were discarded at various Meadowlands dumps. The dumping of household garbage permanently ceased in 1997.

Out of the more than 19,000 acres in the designated Meadowlands "District," which constitutes parts of 14 municipalities, more than 8,400 acres are wetlands and waterways. Most of these are estuarine wetlands associated with the tidal reaches of the Hackensack River and its tributary creeks. These wetlands provide a valuable habitat for a variety of wildlife species. More than 265 species of birds and 30 species of fish have been identified at the preserve. Shrimp, crabs, mussels, clams, and oysters also make their home along the adjoining freshwater marshes.

The Meadowlands area was formed when the Wisconsin glacier receded more than 10,000 years ago. Melted ice created the glacial Lake Hackensack, which eventually joined with the rising waters of the ocean and formed the Hackensack River. The freshwater mixed with salt and created the saltwater and freshwater marshes and meadows known today as the Meadowlands.

As we walked along the park's trails located just outside the environment center, we found ourselves forgetting that we were walking up the steep slopes of an old garbage dump and instead enjoyed the surrounding sights of a wildflower and butterfly meadow with rows of sassafras, daylilies, and sweet gum. Fields of cedar, dogwood, and elderberry trees; eastern coastal grassland prairie; and an evergreen forest also add to the park's amazing landscape.

One of the highlights of the environment center, particularly for children, is the garbage museum. As we entered the dark tunnel of the exhibit, we suddenly found ourselves in the midst of colorful lights illuminating rubber tires, old bicycles, glasses, empty soda bottles, milk cartons, newspapers, and a recording welcoming us to today's trash crisis and its possible solutions. Colorful, interactive displays help deliver the message that we are all part of the trash problem and should all be part of the solution, as well.

Another exhibit area of the museum is the history exhibit, where visitors can walk through time and reflect on the important events in the growth and development of the Meadowlands area. At the end of the history exhibit walkway, visitors are afforded a spectacular panoramic view of the Meadowlands from the glass-enclosed visitors center. The center is built on pilings over the Kingsland Impoundment, providing an ideal location to view the surrounding wildlife feeding and resting in the water below.

In the center's main lobby, a 1,000-gallon replica of an urban salt marsh displays many of the animals common to the Meadowlands, including live grass shrimp, snapping turtles, killifish, and mud and blue crabs. Mounted taxidermal specimens feature a wide variety of animals also common to the area, including raccoons, meadow voles, muskrats, milk snakes, and great egrets.

A bulletin for bird-watchers, located in the lobby, lists information about recent sightings in the area. The Meadowlands is a renowned annual migratory stop for thousands of ducks, geese, and shorebirds, such as herons, sandpipers, gulls, and marsh hawks, once an endangered species.

The Transco Trail, a partial loop around the environment center, provides an opportunity for visitors to explore the recent shore-edge restoration of the area. A portion of this self-guided nature trail is a natural gas pipeline service road that now serves as part of the Marsh Discovery Trail through a cooperative agreement with the Transcontinental Gas Pipe Line Corporation.

Where: Hackensack Meadowlands Environment Center can be reached from State 3, the New Jersey Turnpike, and State 17. Take State 17 south; at the first traffic light, take Polito Avenue and proceed to Valley Brook Avenue. Turn left and follow it to the center. From State 3 east, the Garden State Parkway, and State 21, take State 17 south, exit at the traffic signal, proceed straight on Polito Avenue to Valley Brook Avenue, and turn left into the center.

Hours: The center is open weekdays from 9:00 A.M. to 5:00 P.M., weekends from 10:00 A.M. to 3:00 P.M. The center is closed on holidays.

Admission: $2.00; children under 12 free.

Best time to visit: Try to visit the center on sunny days. The outdoor trails are closed when it rains.

Activities: The center offers group programs and field trips. Preregistration for field trips is accepted by phone on special registration dates. Call for more information. If you are planning a trip in May, the most popular field trip month, book ahead of time. Trips are scheduled on a first-come, first-served basis, and special program fees apply.

Other: Special tours and programs have been developed for small groups and are offered from Monday through Thursday by prior reservation. Plan to spend at least an hour or an hour and a half for each program. The Meadowlands can be wet and muddy, so dress appropriately for outdoor programs.

For more information: Hackensack Meadowlands Development Commission's Environment Center, Two DeKorte Park Plaza, Lyndhurst, NJ 07071. Call 201-460-8300.

4

Central New Jersey

Cheesequake State Park

We set out for the trails of Cheesequake State Park in Middlesex County on a drizzling damp morning, not as unpleasant as it sounds. The majority of the trail we hiked was hooded under a canopy of hardwoods, and the rain seemed to only echo and trickle around us.

We took the green trail, the longest of the three major trails in the park, which carried us along a 90-minute, 3.5-mile loop through a landscape full of surprises. For about 30 minutes, we hiked through glens and uplands until the trail branched off and we found ourselves marching through a cedar and freshwater swamp.

Cheesequake State Park is located near Raritan Bay about five miles south of Perth Amboy, a transitional zone between New Jersey's northern and southern vegetation types. Open fields, saltwater and freshwater marshes, a white cedar swamp, a sample of pinelands, and an outstanding example of a northeastern hardwood forest make up the park's 1,284 acres.

With such a melting pot of habitats within one natural area, the trails throughout the park afford hikers a chance to view a wide variety of plants and wildlife all in a day's visit.

The name Cheesequake originates from the Lenni-Lenape Indians, who once frequented the area to hunt and fish. Evidence of Native American occupation in the area dates back 5,000 years before Henry Hudson sailed into Raritan Bay in 1609.

The park offers a variety of recreational activities for all seasons, including fishing in the trout-stocked Hooks Creek Lake, hiking the scenic trails, and the summer favorites of picnicking, camping, and swimming. In the fall, visitors can enjoy an excellent display of fall foliage in the park's woodlands, as well as the more subtle display of colors in the freshwater and saltwater marshes.

While on the green trail, we hiked through a typical Pine Barrens forest, then downward to a freshwater swamp, where we saw sweetbay magnolia and red maple in a dense stand of Atlantic white cedar. Rainwater plays an important role in creating this rich fertile environment; as it flows down from the upland forest floors, it collects debris, silt, and nutrients that feed the diverse plant and wildlife.

Red maple and black willow stand among the arrowwood, elderberry, and buttonbush shrubs, and hummingbirds thrive on the bright, plentiful orange flowers of jewelweed that blossom along the swamp in October. The tracks of opossums, raccoons, and chipmunks, as well as those of an occasional white-tailed deer, can be seen along the sandy path, bordered by cinnamon ferns.

More than 186 bird species also have been sighted throughout the park. A checklist to help you identify the different species can be picked up at the park office.

The yellow trail offers a scenic short walk toward Hooks Creek Lake, where pinkster, swamp azalea, and mountain laurel flourish in the spring months. This trail is one of the best places in New Jersey to observe pink lady's slippers.

Where: Cheesequake State Park can be reached from State 34 or the Garden State Parkway via Exit 120.

Hours: The park is open daily year-round. The park interpretive center is open Wednesday through Sunday from 8:30 A.M. to 3:00 P.M.

Admission: Fees of $7.00 per vehicle on weekends and holidays and $5.00 per vehicle on weekdays are charged at the park entrance from Memorial Day weekend through Labor Day.

Best time to visit: Year-round.

Activities: Fishing, picnicking, swimming, hiking, and bicycling are popular. The park contains a hill used extensively for sledding in the winter. Fifty-three family campsites are open year-round and are located in two areas: Gordon Field, accommodating up to 150 campers, and Booth Field, accommodating up to 250 campers. Advance reservations are required. Family campsites with flush toilets are $10.00. Group campsites also are available. Basketball courts are located near the beach complex of Hooks Creek Lake.

Concessions: Located near the beach are parking lots, a bathhouse, and a concession stand offering refreshments, novelties, and beach supplies during the summer season only.

Other: The park's interpretive center is easily accessible from the trail system. Displays and exhibits are featured, as well as scheduled tours and activities arranged through the park office.

For more information: Cheesequake State Park, Matawan, NJ 07747. Call 732-566-2161.

Marquand Park

Marquand Park is a perfect example of the many small municipal parks in New Jersey that have so much to offer. Within its 17 acres in Princeton Borough, Mercer County, are some of the largest and oldest trees of their species in New Jersey, as well as unusual and rare plants from around the world.

Originally part of a 30-acre farm purchased in 1842 by a professor at nearby Princeton University, Marquand Park acquired more and more plants over the years, thanks to the fact that all of its owners were avid horticulturists. Professor Allan Marquand bought the property in 1885, and his wife lived there until her death in 1950. Three years later, the heirs gave 17 acres of the estate to Princeton Borough for use as a public park, playground, and recreational area.

The Marquand Park Foundation oversees the care, maintenance, and planting programs of the park and has published an illustrated, very informative guidebook. Most of the trees and shrubs are numbered, and the guidebook provides the genus and species, common name, a brief description, and cultural requirements for each species, just in case you're thinking about adding it to your backyard.

Included in the park's collections are rare evergreens and the dawn redwood, which was thought to have been extinct until 1944, when it was discovered growing in China. Right at the entrance is New Jersey's largest empress tree, which is native to China and Japan. A wooded area of the park includes huge specimens of American beech, hickory, oaks, maples, and tulip trees, as well as spring wildflowers, rhododendrons, azaleas, and mountain laurels. Some of the oldest trees, many close to 200 years old, can be found here.

By following a gravel trail and a map in the guidebook, you can take a self-guided tour of the park. We visited toward evening and were treated to the sight of several white-tailed deer, which are quite common in the area—too common for the many drivers who have had close encounters with them on the road. You can spend as little as 20 minutes walking along the trail or as much as a couple of hours. We spent more than an hour trying to guess some of the more exotic tree species and then checking the guidebook to see if we were correct. It's a great place to learn more about the rare, unusual, and even more common trees and shrubs.

Where: Marquand Park is located off of U.S. 206 on Lovers Lane, south of the center of Princeton.
Hours: Daily, dawn to dusk.
Admission: Free.
Best time to visit: Mid-May.
Activities: A playground and small ballfield are located at the entrance of the park.
Concessions: None.
Pets: Dogs are permitted on a leash.
Other: A guidebook to the park can be purchased for $5.00 from the Historical Society of Princeton, 158 Nassau Street, Princeton, NJ 08540.
For more information: Princeton Borough Engineering Department, Box 390, Monument Drive, Princeton, NJ 08542. Call 609-497-7634.

The New Jersey State Museum and Planetarium

A visit to the planetarium at the State Museum can be just as useful on future camping trips as trail maps and wildlife handbooks. There's nothing like admiring the brilliant stars of a night sky from the darkness and serenity of the woods, but it's even better when you know what you're seeing.

With the help of the planetarium's state-of-the-art projection equipment and a little of your own imagination, you can explore dazzling displays of the galaxy, watch twilight fade away, search for the first appearance of a star, and journey into the unknown.

We sat in awe as the dome of the planetarium came alive with dazzling images of star clusters, constellations, and the Milky Way, which all seemed to rotate around us thanks to special-effects projectors.

Various programs offer tours of the solar system, featuring identification of planets and constellations, simulation of a flight through the rings of Saturn, the opportunity to view a three-dimensional laser light show, or the simple pleasure of stargazing indoors at more than 6,000 stars in the planetarium's sky.

The planetarium is only one of the many highlights of the New Jersey State Museum in Trenton, which affords countless opportunities to explore the natural world year-round. Not only can you explore the universe, but you can journey back through time and see how the earth was formed more than a billion years ago.

We saw the rare skeletal remains of mastodons, the great Ice Age elephants that once roamed throughout the state. Both of the mounts located in the museum's Hall of Natural History were recovered at sites in Sussex and Warren counties.

Other fossils from a dinosaur extinction boundary site in New Jersey are also displayed in the museum, including a crocodile; a mosasaur, or giant sea lizard; and several sea turtles and snails. If you have any questions about these ancient specimens, you can ask the staff member present at the "Working Scientist" station, who often can be found preparing some of the museum's many fossil displays. Make sure you don't miss the life-size replica of the hadrosaur, the official state dinosaur.

If you're interested in archaeology, the museum features a display on the archaeological record of New Jersey's Native Americans. It explains through a series of stations how archaeologists study the past through excavations and analyses of traces left in the ground for millions of years. You also can visit the New Jersey Delaware Indian room, located on the lower level of the museum, where stone tools, arrowheads, clothing, a dugout canoe, and many other artifacts are displayed.

Also located on the lower level is Neptune's Architects, featuring an impressive display of mollusks from the Atlantic and other oceans, including bivalves, snails, chiton, tusk shells, and nautiloids. These fossils, along with their modern relatives, illustrate how some genera have lived on the earth relatively unchanged for millions of years.

Some exciting changes have taken place over the past several years at the museum. There has been a slow renovation of the Natural History Hall in an effort to present each of New Jersey's diverse physiographic regions in a more interdisciplinary manner. Visitors are not only able to see the many wildlife and plant species of the state, but they also are able to see them as they would appear in their natural habitats.

Where: The New Jersey State Museum and Planetarium is located on West State Street in Trenton and is accessible from State 29 and U.S. 1.

Hours: The museum is open Tuesday through Saturday from 9:00 A.M. to 4:45 P.M. and Sunday from noon to 5:00 P.M. The museum is closed on all major holidays. Planetarium shows are open on weekends only (same hours as museum). School groups can schedule special viewings during the week.

Admission: Museum exhibitions and most of the educational programs are open to the public free of charge. Planetarium shows cost $1.00 per person. Tickets can be purchased 30 minutes before each show at the planetarium's box office. Evening laser concerts are $7.00 per adult, $5.00 for children under 12.

Best time to visit: Year-round.

Activities: Various educational programs are offered at the museum for both adults and children. Family and school groups can plan field trips at the planetarium with advance reservations. Films, concerts, dance programs, and children's theater are all part of the museum's regular activities. In addition, special lectures in fine and decorative arts, archaeology, and natural history are given on selected Sunday afternoons throughout the year.

Concessions: The Museum Shop, located on the first floor, features world handicrafts, jewelry, tapestries, and books. A Children's Shop, located in the planetarium library, is open weekdays but closed on weekends. The Museum Café, operated by the Trenton Bagel Shop on the first floor, offers sandwiches, bagels, and desserts during regular museum hours.

Other: All facilities are wheelchair-accessible. Visitors in wheelchairs can use the elevator to the third floor to see the upper floor of the Decorative and Fine Arts Galleries. Wheelchairs are available free of charge. Free parking is available in Capitol Complex Parking, level 1.

For more information: New Jersey State Museum, 205 West State Street, P.O. Box 530, Trenton, NJ 08625-0530. Call 609-292-6464.

Washington Crossing State Park

More than a half-million people a year visit Washington Crossing State Park, the site where George Washington and the Revolutionary Army made the historic crossing of the Delaware River on Christmas night, 1776. The American troops marched over Continental Lane, a path that winds through almost the entire length of the more than 800-acre park in Mercer County.

The original park was established in 1912, containing 100 acres of land and a scenic overlook to the Delaware River and the famous crossing site. The overlook, surrounded by a stone wall, still exists today and can't be missed as you explore the park's 13 miles of trails.

More than 900 historical artifacts are exhibited at the park's visitors center. Two 18th-century colonial houses, the Ferry House and the Nelson House, are located in the park. They are open to visitors to serve as reminders of the Revolutionary War era.

Although the historical significance of the park draws many visitors, the park's lush natural beauty and wide variety of nature programs and tours offered throughout the year attract a fair share of people, too.

It was a crisp fall morning when we made our way through the colorful trails of the park, well known to the residents of the area for its magnificent display of fall foliage. Red maples, sassafras, sumac, flowering dogwoods, and red oaks gave the park deep shades of ruby, scarlet, and bronze. And the leaves of white ash, tulip trees, and hickories added a deep golden hue.

While walking along the trails, we also saw goldenrod, white asters, ironweed, and the yellow spidery blossoms of witch hazel, all in bloom in the fall.

A great place to learn the different colors and types of trees in the park is the George Washington Memorial Arboretum. Varieties of trees and shrubs, all native to the state, are labeled along a shaded dirt trail.

Many different tours and activities to teach you all about the park's diverse plant and wildlife species are offered through Washington Crossing State Park's new interpretive center, which guides visitors through the park's cultural and natural history.

You can join in on the "Family Nature Walk" tour, explore the park for nocturnal wildlife on the "Night Hike," or learn about Native American housing, food, religion, and folklore during one of the center's group programs.

A special course, "Introduction to Amateur Astronomy," also is offered through the center. The Amateur Astronomers' Association of Princeton maintains the observatory in the park.

The center also features several hands-on exhibits, including a fossil display, donated by one of the park's many dedicated volunteers, Al Alden. The exhibit displays brachiopods and other primitive sea creatures from New Jersey, Tennessee, and Kentucky. Petrified wood and marine mammal bones, corals, fish, fossilized fern leaves, and other plant parts are displayed as well.

While at the center, you can pick up checklists of the different mammals and birds common to the area. More than 120 species of birds are listed, including four species of owls— from the approachable saw-whet owl to the skittish great horned owl.

These nocturnal birds are known to have well-developed family bonds, and they make devoted parents. The mates share in incubation duties, but once the eggs are hatched, the male becomes the sole provider. The park's newsletter related that one male became so obsessed with his food-gathering duty that he barely left room in the nest for his family. Four catfish, two eels, eleven rats, four ruffed grouse, one mouse, one muskrat, one woodcock, and a rabbit were found in his nest.

More than a dozen mammals are also common to the area, such as the opossum, shorttail shrew, raccoon, red and gray fox, woodchuck, meadow vole, cottontail rabbit, and deer.

Washington Crossing Open Air Theater is set in one of the park's most unique and beautiful areas. One thousand seats line a sloping hillside, where spectators can come to enjoy concerts and theatrical and musical performances. The park has three major picnic areas with grills or stone fireplaces, as well as group campsites located in the Phillips Farm area.

Where: Washington Crossing State Park is located on the Delaware River just eight miles north of Trenton and is easily accessible from State 29 and County 546.

Hours: The park is open daily during daylight hours throughout the year. The visitors center and nature center are open Wednesday through Sunday from 9:00 A.M. to 4:00 P.M.

Admission: A $3.00 vehicle fee is charged at the park entrance on weekends and holidays from Memorial Day weekend through Labor Day. Most programs offered by the park's nature center are free, and no advance registration is required. However, some programs require a nominal materials charge and/or advance registration. Attendance is limited and is available on a first-come, first-served basis.

Best time to visit: Year-round.

Activities: Picnicking, camping, fishing, hiking, bicycling, horseback riding, and cross-country skiing are permitted. Call the nature center for regularly scheduled events.

Concessions: None.

Other: The visitors center, open-air theater, Ferry House, campsites, and picnic areas are either completely or partially wheelchair-accessible. A nature study area also includes a trail for the blind.

For more information: Washington Crossing State Park, 355 Washington Crossing–Pennsylvania Road, Titusville, NJ 08560-1517. Call 609-737-0623.

5

Southern New Jersey

The New Jersey State Aquarium

Where else in New Jersey—or any other state, for that matter—can you reach right out and touch a shark? How many of us will ever have the chance to come nose-to-beak with an African penguin?

You can do this and more at the New Jersey State Aquarium, located on the east bank of the Delaware River in Wiggins Waterfront Park, Camden. Opened to the public in February 1992, the aquarium in its first year hosted about 1.2 million visitors. On a single day in March of that year, it drew more than 8,500 visitors. Fortunately, the initial rush has subsided, the lines are more tolerable, and the views are less obstructed by other people.

Once you clear the entrance gate, the first exhibits you'll encounter are the outdoor ones, showing two different New Jersey habitats. The first is a cutaway view of a rushing trout stream, featuring native New Jersey species, including the brook trout, catfish, sunfish, and pickerel, as well as introduced species, such as brown and rainbow trout.

After that, wander over to the seal exhibit, where you can watch both harbor and gray seals at play. A sunken amphitheater and a path leading to ground level offer both underwater and aboveground views into the 170,000-gallon tank, which resembles a sandy shoreline where seals typically might be found. The seals, by the way, are the biggest eaters at the aquarium, each consuming up to 11 pounds of fish a day in the winter. Three times a day, you can watch them being fed. There are also daily seal shows where you can see them perform various behaviors. The rest of the time, it's fun just to watch them frolic in the water or sun themselves on a rock.

The newest outdoor exhibit showcases 15 African penguins in a 17,000-gallon pool area called Inguza Island, named after the African word for penguin. Two feet tall and weighing about six pounds, these birds, known for their donkeylike braying, waddle along their beach or sometimes swim right up to the glass in the pool's underwater viewing areas, kindly offering visitors a close-up view. Their black-and-white coloring serves as a kind of camouflage—their black backside blending into the dark watery environment and protecting them from harm above, and their white underbellies blending in with bright light shining down onto the water, helping to hide them from predators below. African penguins are considered threatened, with their population decreasing by 90 percent in the past 60 years due mainly to commercial overfishing of their food supply, habitat destruction, and oil spills. The aquarium plans to breed their penguins eventually, so these black-and-white waddlers will soon have new friends.

Once you leave the penguins and seals behind and enter the two-story aquarium building, it becomes apparent that you really have entered an undersea world. The first floor's showcase exhibit is Ocean Base Atlantic, featuring a 760,000-gallon "Open Ocean" tank, one of the largest in the country. Through a giant window, you can view two dozen sand tiger and sandbar sharks, giant stingrays, sea turtles, and more than 1,400 other aquatic animals native to North America. If you time it right or call ahead for the schedule, you'll see the sharks being fed—a sight that's sure to make you appreciate the fact you're viewing it from dry land.

If you have children, though, they'll probably want to head straightaway to the "Shark Touch" tank. Here, they can touch the rough skin of harmless small sharks and rays in a special shallow pool and learn more about these creatures from the naturalist on duty.

Moving around the Open Ocean tank, you'll find additional vantage points for exploring different areas of the tank. The largest of these is the Deep Atlantic Theatre, an amphitheater with a two-story window that offers a view of the edge of the continental shelf, where it drops off to immeasurable depths (a replica of the Hudson Canyon off New Jersey's coast). Here, aquarium staffers conduct educational programs several times a day. A big treat for kids is the opportunity to ask questions of divers in the tank, who respond by "scubaphone."

Elsewhere on the first floor, you'll find several smaller exhibits, including those that explore life on a barrier beach or in a Pine Barrens stream, and the history and importance of the Delaware River and Delaware Bay. One of the newer exhibits also depicts a typical Caribbean Beach, featuring horsehoe crabs, pointy Atlantic needlefish, and many more colorful species of fish.

In contrast to the typically dark aquarium atmosphere found on the first floor, the second level features bright, colorful exhibits about fish from around the world. Designed to both entertain and inform, these are hands-on exhibits that are sure to delight kids of all ages.

The main exhibit is "W.O.W.—Weird? or Wonderful?" and there's plenty of both. For example, did you know a chameleon's tongue can measure up to one and a half times its total body length? Ever see a fish with four eyes? How about one with horns that looks like a cow? Well, here you can marvel at the four-eyed fish, cowfish, and plenty of other crazy creatures from all over the world. Most of them have developed their odd appearances or habits to enable them to survive in their environments.

A new Children's Garden, a large interactive garden located adjacent to the aquarium and specially designed to appeal to kids, is scheduled to premiere in summer 1999.

Where: The New Jersey State Aquarium in Camden is easily accessible from major highways in the area. Take I-676 to Mickle Boulevard. The aquarium is on Riverside Drive at the foot of Mickle Boulevard.

Hours: Open daily from 9:30 A.M. to 5:30 P.M. During the winter, hours may be shortened and special admission rates offered, while Sunday hours may be extended during the summer. Closed on New Year's Day, Easter, Thanksgiving, and Christmas.

Admission: $10.95 for adults, $9.45 for students with ID and for senior citizens, and $7.95 for children three to eleven; children under two admitted free. Call 800-616-JAWS with major credit card for reservations. Group rates available. Parking is available in the municipal parking garage across the street.

Best time to visit: To avoid crowds, try to visit on Monday mornings or weekday afternoons. Sunday morning is the slowest time on weekends.

Activities: Daily demonstrations include seal shows, dive shows in the Open Ocean tank, penguin and shark feedings, children's theatre, and regularly scheduled programs in the 220-seat auditorium.

Concessions: The Riverview Café is located on the first floor. Pushcart vendors outside the parking garage offer standard sidewalk food and souvenirs. The Crossroads Café is located across the street.

Other: The "A Shop," a gift shop on the first floor, carries a variety of gift items, including books, cards, T-shirts, caps, and toys. The aquarium is wheelchair-accessible. Strollers are permitted during off-peak periods, but your safest bet is to call ahead. Backpacks are provided free of charge. The last ticket is sold an hour before closing time.

For more information: The New Jersey State Aquarium, 1 Riverside Drive, Camden, NJ 08103. Call 800-616-JAWS.

Cape May County Park/Zoo

If you can't see animals in the wild, the next best thing is the zoo. This particularly well-designed zoo, located on 81 acres within Cape May County's main park, features about 350 animals, birds, and reptiles.

The larger animals are housed in expansive enclosures containing trees and other vegetation, while the paths that wind around the zoo are wide, shaded, and lined with a variety of plants, some of which are labeled. This makes not only for an interesting stroll through the zoo, but a pleasant, uncrowded one as well, particularly during the summer.

As with any zoo, you'll see all kinds of animals here, from Bengal tigers resting in big, grassy enclosures to American alligators slinking off into a pond. We were pleased to note that many exhibits feature viewing windows at a child's eye level so that kids don't need a boost to get a good look at the wildlife. At the large compounds, adults and children can pay 25 cents to view the animals more closely through a viewfinder.

Other animals you can see here include river otters frolicking in the water, prairie dogs, black bears, bobcats, monkeys, camels, lions, American buffalo, and exotic birds. Descriptive signs are posted so you can learn a little more about them.

Zoo officials are working to rebuild their Reptile House, which was destroyed in a fire. The Reptile House is expected to reopen in 1999, once again allowing children to "pet" turtles, lizards, and snakes as they are held by zoo staff. The zoo also recently added an aviary featuring more than 20 birds.

Where: Cape May County Park/Zoo is located at Exit 11 off the Garden State Parkway.

Hours: The zoo is open daily from 10:00 A.M. to 4:45 P.M., except for the Reptile House, which is open daily from 10:00 A.M. to 4:00 P.M.

Admission: Free.

Best time to visit: Year-round.

Activities: The park features a fishing pond, hiking and bicycle trails, and playground equipment. Picnic facilities are available for a small fee. The park closes at dusk.

Concessions: A food stand is located outside the main entrance to the zoo. The zoo also has a gift shop.

Pets: Not permitted.

For more information: Cape May County Park Commission, U.S. 9 and Crest Haven Road, Cape May Court House, Cape May, NJ 08210. Call 609-465-5271.

Leaming's Run Garden and Colonial Farm

If you're going to visit just one of New Jersey's many gardens and arboretums, you wouldn't go wrong in choosing Leaming's Run. With 20 acres of beautiful floral and herb displays and an 18th-century colonial farm hidden amid tall, fragrant pines, the garden's winding paths offer a delightful experience for the entire family.

This garden in Cape May is designed for leisurely walks along 25 theme-colored displays. A winding path will lead you from the vibrant summer blossoms, banana peppers, and gladioli of the Yellow Garden to such serene settings as the Reflection Garden, where the surrounding flora can be seen mirrored on a pond's surface.

As the largest annual garden in the country, with more than 10,000 annual flowers replanted seasonally, Leaming's Run is enough to impress most garden enthusiasts.

Signs along the sandy path invite visitors to freely explore the garden's natural landscape, carrying messages such as, "It's O.K. to Walk on the Grass" and "Look Back," so that you don't overlook some of the garden's most impressive views.

After traveling past the Blue and White Garden, where morning glories can be seen in full bloom during the early hours of spring and summer, and visiting the English Cottage Garden, a haven for resident hummingbirds in August, we passed under an ivy-covered trellis and found ourselves stepping back into early colonial history.

Nestled in the garden's thriving natural landscape is a reproduction of the original colonial farm built when Thomas Leaming first settled his 320 acres of land in the early 1700s. The reproduction of the one-room log cabin where the original Leaming lived temporarily until the main house was built, brings to life the daily routines and hardships faced by the whalers who first settled in Cape May County.

Dried beans hang from the cabin's rafters, a colorful patchwork quilt brightens the rustic setting, and an ivory ceramic washbasin sits close to the fireplace. When we entered the log cabin, with its simple furnishings and fresh-air smell mixed with the lingering scent of fire kindling, we couldn't help but feel as though we had walked back in time.

Outside the cabin, tobacco and cotton grow just as they did in Leaming's time.

A vegetable garden, filled with crops brought by the first settlers for survival, is planted with corn, root crops, wheat, and sugar cane—all grown for home use. Various herbs are planted close to the cabin; these were essential to adding variety to the settlers' limited diet.

Children will enjoy the farm's stable and pens, where farm animals such as turkeys, roosters, hens, and the ancient breed of Silver Spangled Hamburg chickens can be seen.

Before moving on to the garden's many other beautiful displays ahead, take a moment to read the one-page copy of Leaming's diary posted outside the cabin. The copy, dated 1674–1707, offers a quick glimpse of Leaming's whaling adventures and some of the hardships and joys of colonial living. It also gives a little insight into the type of early settlers who landed in Cape May, mostly seamen making their living off the once abundant whale population found along the Jersey shore.

One of the most picturesque spots of the garden, great for picture-taking and viewing the resident hummingbirds, is the Serpentine Garden. The garden is planted in a winding design that allows a fuller view of the fiery red salvia that leads all the way up to the garden's gazebo. We stood for a few moments, taking in the excellent view from the gazebo's platform, where the bright flowers, a wooden footbridge, and a pond full of blooming lily pads could be seen and enjoyed.

At the end of the path is the cooperage, a charming antique barn Leaming built in 1706 when he retired from whaling and became a cooper, or barrelmaker. The cooperage, which has been converted into a flower and gift shop, features a colorful collection of dried flower baskets similar to the ones used by early settlers to add color to their homes. A variety of dried materials, many grown in the gardens behind the barn, are available for making your own dried arrangements.

Where: Leaming's Run is located on the west side of U.S. 9 north in Swainton, Cape May County. Take Exit 13 of the Garden State Parkway to U.S. 9. Proceed one mile north to the garden entrance on the left.

Hours: Open daily from 9:30 A.M. to 5:00 P.M., May 15 through October 20.

Admission: $5.00 for adults, $1.00 for children six to twelve years old. Children under six are admitted free. Annual tickets are available for unlimited visits for $12.00.

Best time to visit: Summer and fall.

Concessions: The cooperage gift shop is open from May 15 until fall and can be visited apart from the gardens via its entrance on Route 9 north. Hours are daily from 10:00 A.M. to 5:00 P.M.

For more information: Leaming's Run Garden and Colonial Farm, 1845 U.S. 9 North, Cape May Court House, Cape May, NJ 08210. Call 609-465-5871.

6

The Pine Barrens

The Pine Barrens, encompassing more than one million acres in southern New Jersey, is the largest tract of open land on the mid-Atlantic coast. It spreads across seven counties and accounts for more than 20 percent of the total land area in New Jersey, a figure made all the more amazing since New Jersey is the most densely populated state in the nation.

Miles of sandy roads traverse the predominantly pitch pine forests that stretch as far as the eye can see. You'll also find several species of oak trees, as well as cedar and hardwood swamps bordering the many streams and rivers. A 12,000-acre area contains "pygmy forest," a distinctive stand of dwarf pine and oak trees no taller than 11 feet.

The Pine Barrens, so-named because of its largely infertile, sandy, acidic soil, is far from being barren. This wilderness-like area is home to more than 350 species of birds, mammals, reptiles, and amphibians. Of these 350 species, more than 30 are either threatened or endangered, including the Pine Barrens tree frog and the corn and pine snakes. More than 50 plant species found here, such as the curly grass fern, also are listed as endangered.

The first inhabitants of the Pine Barrens were the Lenni-Lenape Indians, who hunted and fished here while on their way to and from the shore. Loggers were the first permanent settlers, supplying shipyards and nearby towns with pine and cedar lumber for years before, during, and after the American Revolution.

Several other industries flourished throughout the years, including glassmaking, paper production, and bog iron. Today, existing industries include recreation, sand and gravel mining, and cranberry and blueberry harvesting. New Jersey's cranberry production, which is third in the nation, is carried out predominantly in the Pine Barrens of Burlington County. You can see some of these cranberry farms along Route 563 south of Chatsworth.

To protect the Pine Barrens from unrestricted development, Congress in 1978 created the Pinelands National Reserve, the first in the country. The Pinelands Commission, a state agency, was established a year later and charged with evaluating the area's resources and planning how to balance protection with new development. In 1983, the United Nations recognized the importance of the Pine Barrens by designating the region an International Biosphere Reserve. These reserves are protected areas established to conserve species and natural communities and to further research ways to use these areas without degrading them.

Underlying the sandy soil throughout much of the Pine Barrens is the Cohansey Aquifer, containing an estimated 17 trillion gallons of pure water, or enough water to cover the entire state with 10 feet of water. This aquifer provides the water supply for area residents and industries and feeds most of the area's streams.

Every year, wildfires rage through parts of the Pine Barrens. To some extent, they are part of the area's natural life cycle. The pitch pine is a prime example. Its cones are sealed with a resin that is broken only by the type of high temperatures generated by forest fires. When the seal breaks, the seeds are dispersed and new growth follows.

Forest fires, of course, can threaten both life and property. The state forest service annually burns between 10,000 and

15,000 acres a year here under controlled conditions to reduce the accumulations of pine needles and leaves, prime fuel for wildfires. Visitors should be careful to observe fire-safety precautions, especially during the wildfire-prone spring.

You could spend an entire lifetime exploring the Pine Barrens. Some of its furthest reaches, including Island Beach State Park and the Edwin B. Forsythe National Wildlife Refuge, often are identified more with the shore area, so we have opted to include them in the Jersey Shore chapter. In the pages that follow, we provide a few good starting points for exploring the natural and cultural history of what generally is considered to be "the heart" of the Pine Barrens.

Wharton State Forest

Wharton State Forest is well known to South Jersey schoolchildren and history buffs as the home of Batsto, a historic 19th-century Pine Barrens village. But there are plenty of natural attractions here as well.

Wharton, which contains more than 110,000 acres in Atlantic, Burlington, and Camden counties, is the largest state-owned tract of land. It offers opportunities to canoe some of the most popular Pine Barrens rivers and explore more than 500 miles of sandy roads and trails.

Batsto once was the site of a thriving bog iron industry. Founded in 1766, Batsto supplied wartime products, such as munitions and camp kettles, to the Continental Army during the American Revolution. Later, it was noted for its production of pig iron, cast-iron water pipe, and various specialty castings. After the demise of the iron industry in 1855, Batsto became known for its production of window glass until that industry, too, died out.

Joseph Wharton, a Philadelphia industrialist and financier,

purchased Batsto in 1876 and developed it as a gentleman's farm, enlarging the mansion, building a sawmill, and clearing vast areas of land to cultivate cranberries and other crops. He continued to purchase properties in South Jersey with the intent of damming the streams and rivers and selling the water to Camden and Philadelphia, but his goal was never realized. When he died in 1909, his landholdings totaled approximately 96,000 acres. The state purchased the property in the mid-1950s and named the forest after Wharton, whose original 96,000 acres make up its core.

Today, school groups and other visitors can tour Batsto Village to learn about the industry, commerce, and agriculture that once thrived here. Among the 33 historic buildings and structures here are the gristmill, sawmill, general store, post office, and village houses, as well as the mansion. Guided tours of the mansion are offered at scheduled times.

After touring the village, don't miss the short nature trail along Batsto Pond. Batsto Pond was created in 1766 by the damming of the Batsto River to provide water power for the Batsto sawmill, gristmill, and bog iron furnace. In spring and summer, you're likely to see turtles sunning themselves on the logs in the pond. Harmless northern water snakes also are common here.

A trail guide, available at the visitors center or at the start of the trail, will help in identifying the plants found along the way, such as the golden heather, the bracken fern, and typical Pine Barrens trees. Golden heather, also called Pine Barrens heather, is a shrubby, low plant with small, bright yellow flowers that bloom in mid-May. The bracken fern, the most common fern in the Pine Barrens forests, can be recognized by its large size, very wide fronds, and location in dry habitats.

You won't see many animals along this walk, other than an occasional bird, squirrel, or fence lizard. If you've set out early in the morning, you may catch a glimpse of a white-tailed deer, the only large mammal found in the Pine Barrens. Most other mammals are nocturnal and shy away from areas like this where human encounters are possible.

In the western section of Wharton, the Atsion Recreation Area is especially popular with families during the summer. One of two developed camping areas in Wharton, Atsion offers swimming in the designated bathing area, picnic facilities, a playground, and more opportunities to explore Pine Barrens trails. Nine cabins, accommodating from four to eight people, are situated along the northern shore of the lake.

Where: Wharton State Forest is located about 20 miles northwest of Atlantic City and is accessible from the Atlantic City Expressway, the Garden State Parkway, and U.S. 30 and U.S. 206.

Hours: The Atsion park office is open daily from 8:30 A.M. to 4:00 P.M. The Batsto grounds are open daily from dawn to dusk. Batsto's visitors center, which serves as the main park office, is open daily from 9:00 A.M. to 4:30 P.M. Closed on Thanksgiving, Christmas, and New Year's Day.

Admission: $3.00 parking fee on weekends at Batsto from Memorial Day weekend through Labor Day. Mansion tour fees are $2.00 for ages twelve and up and $1.00 for ages six to eleven. Children under six are admitted free. Atsion fees are $5.00 per car on weekdays and $7.00 per car on weekends and holidays for use of the lake area during the summer. There is no daily fee after Labor Day.

Best time to visit: Year-round.

Activities: Hiking, canoeing, and horseback riding are popular.

Concessions: Batsto has a picnic area and there is a food concession at Atsion Lake.

Pets: Pets are not permitted in campsites.

Other: Year-round camping is available. Facilities range from campsites with fire rings, picnic tables, flush toilets, and hot showers to wilderness sites accessible only by hiking, horseback, or canoe. Developed camping areas are located at Atsion and Godfrey Bridge. Camping is by permit only. Campsites with flush toilets are $10.00 per night. Sites without flush toilets and wilderness campsites are $8.00 per night. Group campsites and cabins are available.

To reserve one of the Atsion cabins, contact the Atsion park office. The camping facilities here are partially wheelchair-accessible.

Batsto offers interpretive programs daily during the summer season. The visitors center is barrier-free.

For more information: Wharton State Forest, RD #9 Batsto, Hammonton, NJ 08037. Call 609-561-0024. Historic Batsto Village, Wharton State Forest, RD #9 Batsto, Hammonton, NJ 08037. Call 609-561-3262. Atsion Office, 744 U.S. 206, Shamong, NJ 08088. Call 609-268-0444.

Canoeing the Wading River

As we paddled our way along the Wading River, we marveled once again at the beauty of the tea-colored water. It was as though someone had tossed thousands of copper pennies to the bottom of the river, where they glowed in the midday sun.

We had canoed this river before and, on this early fall day, decided on an easy, four-hour trip from Hawkins Bridge to Beaver Branch. Though this is the most popular river in the Pine Barrens and it often is well used during the summer, we spotted only one other canoe during the entire stretch on this early fall day.

Canoeing the rivers of the Pine Barrens can be one of the best ways to spot animals and to enjoy the scenic beauty of this wild area. As you paddle along and around each curve, a new tranquil scene unfolds before your eyes. We spotted a number of turtles sunning themselves on tree limbs jutting out of the water. Occasionally, we passed too close to the riverbank and were forced to duck under low-hanging tree branches along the shore. But even close-up brushes with the riverbank can offer delights in the form of wild cranberries and blueberries that grow abundantly there.

There are short, sandy beaches where you can stop for lunch and enjoy the serenity of the river. As you sit back and relax, you may wonder what causes the dark, tea-colored appearance of not only the Wading River, but all Pine Barrens waters. It's due to the iron and other organic contents that leach out of the highly acidic soil found in the Pine Barrens.

This section of the Wading River is part of one of four major canoe trails that travel through Wharton State Forest and are popular with canoeists. Entry and exit points are situated for trips of varying lengths. Designated campsites are located on all but the Oswego River. If you plan to camp overnight, you must obtain a permit from the forest office. The canoe trails are:

West Branch of the Wading River from Speedwell to Beaver Branch or to Wading River Bridge. The run takes approximately seven to twelve hours. Camping is permitted at Hawkin Bridge, Godfrey Bridge, and Bodine Field, where sanitary facilities and drinking water are available.

Mullica River from Atsion Lake to Pleasant Mills near Batsto. This run takes approximately eight hours. You can camp at Mullica River Camp. Sanitary facilities and drinking water are available, but motor vehicles are not permitted.

Batsto River from Hampton Furnace to Quaker Bridge to Batsto Lake. Travel time is approximately seven hours. One campsite is available at Lower Forge. Sanitary facilities are available, but there is no drinking water, and motor vehicles are not permitted.

Oswego River from Lake Oswego (in Penn State Forest) to Harrisville Lake. This run takes about four hours. No campsites are available.

A list of canoe rental facilities is available from the Pinelands Commission, P.O. Box 7, New Lisbon, NJ 08064. Call 609-894-9342. You should call these rental facilities for reservations during the busy summer months. Most places offer drop-off and pick-up at designated spots.

Lebanon State Forest

Named after the Lebanon Glass Works, a thriving Pine Barrens industry in the mid-1800s, this state forest in Burlington and Ocean Counties features dense stands of Atlantic white cedar and a variety of typical Pine Barrens plant species, including rare orchids, sundews, pitcher plants, pyxie moss, and sand myrtle.

Whitesbog Village, located at the northern end of this more than 34,000-acre forest, was the birthplace of the cultivated blueberry and once was the largest cranberry farm in the state. You can tour the historic village, where you can see abandoned cranberry bogs, as well as modern bogs that are leased for cultivation. The buildings are closed to the public, but there are plans to eventually restore them.

The Batona Trail, which stretches for approximately 50 miles through Pine Barrens wilderness, begins here in Leba-

Cranberry Bog, Lebanon State Forest

non at Ong's Hat, continuing through Batsto and Wharton State Forest into Bass River State Forest. Its signature pink blazes guide hikers on a flat path that can be enjoyed by trekkers of all ability levels. Along the way, you can see orchids, huckleberries, deer, hawks, and a variety of other plants and animals.

We hiked a portion of the Batona Trail along Lebanon's Pakim Pond. The trail coincides with part of a self-guided nature tour around the pond. A copy of the nature guide and a map of the Batona Trail are available in the park office.

A popular recreation area today, Pakim Pond was a working cranberry bog until the 1930s. Once the bog was abandoned, pitch pine, red maple, and Atlantic white cedar began to invade the wetland. The area would have reverted back to a cedar swamp had it not been for a family of industrious beavers that built a dam that reflooded the area and killed most of the trees, creating a marsh. The marsh attracts carpenter frogs; spotted, painted, and red-bellied turtles; and a variety of birds, such as green herons, great blue herons, kingfishers, mallards, black ducks, and wood ducks.

Only a few species of fish can live in the acidic Pine Barrens waters. The smaller ones, the banded sunfish, swamp darter, and mudminnows, are eaten by the larger redfin pickerel, chain pickerel, and bullhead catfish. The pickerel and catfish are the only game fish native to the Pine Barrens waters.

Along the way, we stopped to sample some wild blueberries growing along the edge of the trail, while farther ahead, we noticed a red-bellied turtle sunning itself on a log. If you look carefully out at the water, you may spot a bladderwort, an insect-eating plant. The bladderwort, which has tiny yellow flowers, traps its food with small, insect-catching sacs located on its underwater leaves.

Beavers also are common in the area. If you look carefully, you may see beaver cuttings and evidence of dam-building activities along the edges of the pond.

While the blue-blazed nature trail will take you back to Pakim Pond, the pink-blazed Batona Trail continues through Lebanon State Forest on its way to Wharton State Forest. The Batona Trail crosses a number of roads and can be reached by car at many points, so you can enjoy shorter hikes, such as this one. If you prefer an overnight outing, camping is permitted in designated areas with a valid permit. Check with the park office at the area where you'll be staying.

Where: Lebanon State Forest is located in Burlington and Ocean Counties and is easily accessible from State 70 and State 72.

Hours: The park office is open weekdays from 8:00 A.M. to 4:30 P.M. Hours may vary on weekends.

Admission: Free.

Best time to visit: Year-round.

Activities: Hiking and horseback riding are popular.

Concessions: None.

Pets: Pets are not permitted in campsites.

Other: Picnic facilities are available here, as are group campsites and cabins. Campsites, at $10.00 per night, include rest rooms with hot showers, a laundry room, and drinking water.

For more information: Lebanon State Forest, P.O. Box 215, New Lisbon, NJ 08064. Call 609-726-1191.

Double Trouble State Park

Leave it to us to get lost in the smallest state park that we visited during our most recent tour of the Pine Barrens. We were too busy taking in the close-up views of nature along the park's intimate winding trails to realize we had somehow wandered off the beaten path.

We started out on the right track as we explored the remnants of the park's once-productive cranberry village. However, as we found ourselves stepping back in time through the park's rich history, we also found ourselves stepping in the wrong direction. We found our way soon enough, most likely seeing more of the surrounding area than if we had followed the guided trail from the start.

The early history of the cranberry industry has been preserved at this state park in Ocean County, which features cranberry bogs that are cultivated to this day.

A sawmill and lumber industry that operated here from the 1700s into the early 1900s harvested the surrounding Atlantic white cedar swamp for timber. Cranberry vines were planted as the timber was removed, and in 1909 the entire area became the Double Trouble (cranberry) Company. In 1964, the state purchased the operation, leasing some of the bogs for cultivation to maintain them in operating condition.

There are many legends about how Double Trouble earned its name, but most experts believe that it came about with the start of the cranberry industry. The earliest story attributes the name to Thomas Potter, who supposedly uttered the words "double trouble" after spring rains twice washed out the dam. Another legend points to local muskrats, which caused frequent leaks by gnawing at the dam. When a leak was discovered, someone would yell, "Here's trouble," and the workmen would rush to repair the leak. One day, two breaks were discovered and one workman heard the owner shout, "Here's double trouble."

The Double Trouble Historic District is located on an area of high ground between two great bogs, the Gowdy Bog to the east and Old Mill Pond Bog, now dry, to the west. Within the district are the remains of many of the structures of the cranberry village. Tours of the village, including the sawmill and sorting and packing house, are conducted throughout the summer. Contact the park for the schedule.

The cranberry sorting and packing house, restored in 1997, was in operation from 1909 to 1916. It contains three intact cranberry separators, machines with systems of conveyor belts to help with manual sorting of the cranberries. The berries, scooped by hand, were taken by elevator to the third floor of the sorting house and poured into the tops of the separators. The separators, each a system of belts, bins, and rollers, brought the berries down to the second floor, providing a moving ribbon. Women seated on either side manually separated the ripe berries from the green ones, twigs, and leaves. The clean berries were then moved to the packing area for boxing and shipping.

The village also includes a tiny, one-room schoolhouse, the oldest remaining structure; a general store; bunkhouse; cookhouse; sawmill; and residences.

After walking around the village, head back toward the office buildings to the start of the 1.25-mile nature trail. A box here contains copies of the trail guide, which you are encouraged to drop off at the end of your walk. This trail will take you on a 30-minute walk during which you can see active cranberry bogs.

Cranberries thrive here because they need plenty of clean water. In the winter, the bogs are flooded to protect the plants from frost, while in the fall, water is needed to harvest the berries. When shaken from the vine, the berries float to the surface of the water, where they can be scooped up by machines. If you visit in late September or early October, you can watch workers flood the bogs and harvest the cranberries.

With the help of the trail guide, you can identify common Pine Barren trees along the way, such as the pitch pine, which has needles in clusters of three and cones with sharp spines, and the Atlantic white cedar, once an important wood for boatbuilding. Pitcher plants, which lure, trap, and digest small insects, also can be seen here.

Where: Double Trouble State Park is located on Pinewald-Keswick Road, at the intersection with Double Trouble Road, off Exit 80 west of the Garden State Parkway.

Hours: Daily, dawn to dusk.

Admission: Free.

Best time to visit: Late September through early October for cranberry harvest.

Activities: No picnic facilities or camping.

Concessions: None.

Pets: Leashed pets are permitted.

Other: Canoeing is popular on Cedar Creek. You can make arrangements through one of the local private canoe rental facilities. Parking at this state park is limited.

For more information: Double Trouble State Park, P.O. Box 175, Bayville, NJ 08721. Call 732-341-6662.

Greenwood Wildlife Management Area

If you want to hear a Pine Barrens tree frog, one of your best bets is to visit Webbs' Mill Bog Cedar Swamp, located in the northern area of this 28,172-acre wildlife management area in Ocean County.

A boardwalk and trail will take you over a Pine Barrens bog that supports a variety of plants, including rare curly grass ferns, sundews, and pitcher plants. The area is part of a cedar swamp that had been cleared and is in the process of regeneration. To help protect the vegetation here, be sure to stay on the boardwalk.

The best time to hear the mating call of the endangered Pine Barrens tree frog is on a warm, humid, or rainy night in May and June. The tree frog, which is a bright-green color with lavender striping, is only about 1.5 inches high and is very difficult to spot. Listen for its "quonk-quonk" call. If it's near the boardwalk, shine your flashlight in the direction of the sound and you may be lucky enough to catch a glimpse of this elusive creature.

Also in this area, but a good distance away, is a den for hibernating timber rattlesnakes. Robins also can be found in the cedar swamp during the winter.

Where: Greenwood Wildlife Management Area is located on County 539 south of Whiting. From the intersection of County 539 and State 72, drive 6.2 miles north and park by the bridge that crosses Webb's Mill Branch. The boardwalk is on the opposite side of the road from the sign for Greenwood Wildlife Management Area, a few yards toward State 72. Look carefully amid the vegetation at roadside for the trail leading down into the swamp area. A new parking area and trail entrance are planned. Signs will be posted on County 539 to direct visitors there.

Hours: Daily from 5:00 A.M. to 9:00 P.M.

Admission: Free.

Best time to visit: May and June are the best times to hear the Pine Barrens tree frog.

Activities: Hunting and wildlife watching are popular activities.

Concessions: None.

Pets: Pets should be leashed.

For more information: The Division of Fish, Game and Wildlife, P.O. Box 400, Trenton, NJ 08625. Call 609-259-2132.

7

The Jersey Shore

Sandy Hook

If you like to combine your appreciation of nature with the opportunity to learn more about our country's history, this is a great place to do it.

Sandy Hook is a long, slender barrier beach peninsula that forms one of two "arms" of land that stretch out toward each other at the entrance to New York Harbor. Millions of immigrants entered the country through this natural gateway, which inspired the national parksite's name—Gateway National Recreation Area.

The Gateway National Recreation Area, which includes 26,000 acres of land and water, was created by Congress in 1972 as one of the first large urban parks to be managed by the National Park Service. It contains three units: Sandy Hook in New Jersey and the Jamaica Bay–Breezy Point and Staten Island units in New York.

With the ocean on one side and Sandy Hook Bay on the other, Sandy Hook stretches almost 6.5 miles into lower New York Harbor. Within the more than 1,600-acre park are many opportunities to explore its ocean and bayside beaches, dunes, salt marshes, and hiking trails, as well as to take in its long-standing military history.

Sandy Hook Beach

Sandy Hook is well known for having one of the largest stands of holly on the East Coast, containing some trees up to 150 years old. The holly trees are located within a maritime forest, which also includes Eastern red oak and wild black cherry trees. Located near Horseshoe Cove on the bay side of Sandy Hook, this forest is not open to the public, except through scheduled guided tours that are offered during fall, winter, and spring. There are also other trails that offer visitors glimpses of the holly stands here.

One is the Old Dune Trail, a one-mile loop that travels from forest to dune communities. It begins at the Sandy Hook Visitor Center opposite Spermaceti Cove, where you can pick up a trail guide and other park information, and ends on the beach in sight of the building. Along the way, you'll enter part of the holly forest, where the trees thrive in the salt air and sandy soil.

If you're walking along this trail during the fall, you might be tempted to sample the bright red fruit of the prickly pear cactus. The prickly pear stores waters in its fleshy pads, which are protected from animals by hairlike spines. If you want to taste one of its fruits, peel off the pear's skin carefully to remove the spines. We thought we were careful, but an hour later we were squinting our eyes trying to find the nearly invisible spines that were embedded in our fingers.

There are a few other trails you can explore, too, and the visitors center staff can direct you to the starting points. The South Beach Dune Trail extends north from the fishing beach for about a mile, carrying you through the holly forest up the middle of Sandy Hook. Another, known informally as the "Fisherman's Trail," starts at the north end of Sandy Hook near Area K and goes past a freshwater pond, which attracts migrating birds. To see ospreys and snowy egrets, try the boardwalks over the salt marsh at both Spermaceti and Horseshoe Coves.

Sandy Hook is located along the Atlantic Flyway, a major migratory route for many bird species. The hawk migration draws birders in early spring, while later in the spring and in the fall you can see migrating songbirds.

That Sandy Hook has remained undeveloped is in large part due to its use for many years by the military. The Army first fortified it in the War of 1812 and later tested weapons at the Sandy Hook Proving Ground. Fort Hancock was established in 1895, the last of several forts erected here to protect the shipping channels into New York Harbor. It served this role until it was closed in 1974. Many of the fort's buildings are in use today by environmental and educational groups. You can learn more about the military history here by visiting the Fort Hancock Museum, which is in the old post jail, and History House, a restored home on "Officer's Row."

After leaving Sandy Hook, you might want to stop at the Twin Lights Historic Site. Located here is the Navesink Light Station, also known as Twin Lights for its two lighthouse towers. Situated on one of the highest points on the Atlantic coast, lighthouses here have guided mariners into New York Harbor since 1828. You can tour the museum, which features exhibits on lighthouse lenses, the U.S. Life Saving Service, and the Marconi wireless telegraph, as well as climb to the top of the north lighthouse tower for a view of Sandy Hook, the Atlantic Ocean, the New York skyline, and the coast of Long Island.

Where: Sandy Hook is located off the Garden State Parkway. Take Exit 117 (or U.S. 9 and State 35 south) to State 36 east to Sandy Hook. To reach Twin Lights from Sandy Hook, take State 36 west across the Highlands Bridge. Turn right at the west side of the bridge and proceed downhill to Bay Avenue. Turn right beneath the bridge and take an immediate right onto Highland Avenue (you have made a U-turn under the bridge). Cross over Portland Road and continue on Highland Avenue to the sign for the Twin Lights State Historic Site. Make a left and continue up the road into the Twin Lights parking lot.

Hours: The park is open daily from sunrise to sunset. The visitors center is open daily from 10:00 A.M. to 5:00 P.M. Sandy Hook Museum and History House are open weekends from 1:00 P.M. to 5:00 P.M. year-round. Twin Lights is open daily from 10:00 A.M. to 5:00 P.M. from Labor Day through Memorial Day. The rest of the year it's open from Wednesday through Sunday, 10:00 A.M. to 5:00 P.M. The grounds are open until sunset.

Admission: Parking fees at designated beach areas are $10.00 per car on weekends and holidays, $8.00 per car on weekdays, from Memorial Day through Labor Day. Admission to Twin Lights is free.

Best time to visit: Summer for swimming, spring and fall for bird-watching; spring, summer, and fall for fishing.

Activities: Swimming (lifeguards on duty daily from 10:00 A.M. to 6:00 P.M., from Memorial Day weekend through Labor Day), hiking, fishing on unguarded beaches, birding, and windsurfing are popular.

Concessions: Food, drinks, snacks, and beach supplies are sold along certain areas of Sandy Hook beach from April through October, and the visitors center has a bookstore. Twin Lights sells souvenirs and books.

Pets: Pets are not allowed on ocean beaches from March 15 through Labor Day to protect nesting shorebirds. Otherwise, pets must be leashed at all times. Pets at Twin Lights also must be leashed.

Other: Tours and talks on the history and ecology of Sandy Hook, as well as Fort Hancock, are offered throughout the year. A calendar of events is posted on all bulletin boards. The ranger station is staffed 24 hours a day. Interpreter-led tours for groups are available at Twin Lights with at least two weeks' advance reservations.

For more information: Superintendent, Sandy Hook Unit, Gateway National Recreation Area, P.O. Box 530, Fort Hancock, NJ 07732. Call 732-872-5970 (visitors center). Twin Lights Historic Site, Lighthouse Road, Highlands, NJ 07732. Call 732-872-1814.

Island Beach State Park

Island Beach State Park is one of the few remaining undeveloped barrier beaches on the North Atlantic. A popular swimming and sunbathing spot, the park draws 10,000 to 15,000 visitors per day during the summer. But if you've never ventured more than a few yards from the public beach, you've been missing quite a lot.

While most visitors are familiar with the designated ocean bathing beach in the central part of the park, Island Beach State Park also offers opportunities to explore sand dune, saltwater marsh, and freshwater bog habitats, as well as observe their respective plant and animal communities.

The best place to start exploring these natural areas is at the new park interpretive museum, which is housed in a renovated historic Coast Guard building. Exhibits on the park's history, wildlife, vegetation, and maritime cycles are displayed, as well as a hands-on herbarium, containing a complete set of flowers and other plant life found throughout the park.

In the summer, the staff here conduct a variety of nature-related tours and activities, including bird walks; beach area nature walks for both adults and children; canoe trips; seining (netting) demonstrations; and theme tours focusing on history, geology, plants, and birds.

We and a handful of other visitors met up here with naturalist Francis O'Brien for one of the center's late summer nature walks through the northern area, also known as the botanical preserve. We followed a path along a hardwood forest, which features oak, maple, cedar, holly, and black cherry trees, taking note of the "pruning" effect of salt spray on the trees in this park. When the spray hits the sand dunes, the salt from the ocean is carried by the wind, builds up on tree leaves, and ultimately suffocates them. Eventually, the dead branches break off, giving the trees in the park a rounded shape.

We paused to sample the sweet, blue fruit of the beach plum and continued walking toward Barnegat Bay. The bay is a shallow body of water, with an average depth of 10 feet.

Standing at the edge, O'Brien pointed out eel grass that had washed up. Eel grass is a flowering plant that grows in the bay. In the early 1920s, it was harvested, dried, and used for house insulation, furniture stuffing, and packing material for shipping. It has no odor when dry, but gives off the stench of rotten eggs when wet.

We backtracked to the road to explore the dune community behind the nature center. Sand dunes are critical to the survival of the park, providing protection from wind and surf erosion. The sand is held in place by beach grass, which has deep roots that may extend as far as 20 feet to the base of the dune. Though beach grass is extremely resistant to storms and temperature extremes, it can be damaged easily by human activity. Walking or driving on the dunes exposes the roots and destroys the beach grass. As a result, the dunes are weakened and the sand is blown away. Therefore, it is important that you stay on designated trails and heed the signs telling you to keep off the dunes.

Hudsonia, also known as beach heather, is one of the plants that thrives in this type of sandy community. In the winter, it has a gray appearance, but when it blooms around Memorial Day weekend, it resembles a carpet of gold. Since its surface roots give off a toxin, little else will grow around it. Its carpetlike appearance and extensive root system help hold the sand in place, so you should be careful not to disturb these areas, too.

After the tour ended, O'Brien pointed us toward two spots of special interest in the southern natural area. The first, at parking area A-13, is a self-guided trail through a bog, or freshwater community. In this area, you'll see cranberries, sphagnum moss, and ferns. Among the park animals you might spot here are foxes, raccoons, squirrels, rabbits, weasels, and several species of turtles, as well as a variety of woodland birds.

A quarter-mile walk from parking area A-20 will take you to the Spizzle Creek Bird Blind. At the start of the path, a sign cautions visitors to use insect repellent from June to September. Don't ignore it. We did and were still comparing mosquito-bite welts on our legs a week later. But the serene view from the bird blind made it all worthwhile.

The blind looks out over a saltwater marsh, where two ospreys were calmly perched on nesting platforms to our right. The installation of such artificial nesting platforms here and elsewhere in the state has helped the osprey population rebound from its former endangered status. The park has 22 nesting towers and supports the largest concentration of active osprey nesting sites in New Jersey.

Adding to the tranquil scene before us was a snowy egret, wading at water's edge. Other birds you're likely to spot here include the great blue heron, great egret, green heron, glossy ibis, black skimmer, and cormorant. Be sure to bring binoculars for close-up views. In fall and winter, wading birds are replaced by waterfowl, including black and bufflehead ducks, and Atlantic brant.

Where: Island Beach State Park is located off Exit 82 east of the Garden State Parkway. Take State 37 east, cross the bridge over Barnegat Bay, remaining in right lanes, and follow signs to Island Beach State Park.

Hours: The park is open daily year-round from 8:00 A.M. to dusk. The park office generally is open daily from 8:00 A.M. to 4:30 P.M. The nature center is open from April 1 through October 31. Hours can vary, but usually are Wednesday through Sunday from 9:00 A.M. to 4:00 P.M. Public programs are offered on weekends in spring and fall, and daily during the summer. Some programs require preregistration through the park office.

Admission: $7.00 per car on weekends and holidays, $6.00 per car on weekdays, from Memorial Day through Labor Day. During the off-season, admission is $4.00 per vehicle.

Best time to visit: Spring for songbird migration, fall for colorful foliage. In late September, also look for monarch butterflies that congregate here on their way to South America.

Activities: Horseback riding is permitted from October 1 through April 30. A parking area is designated for horse trailers during this time, and advance reservations are required. Surfing is limited to the extreme southern end of the designated bathing area. Scuba diving is permitted along 2.5 miles of ocean beach just north of the Barnegat Inlet. Scuba divers must register at the park office prior to their first dive each year. Picnicking is permitted on the open ocean beach. Grills may be used on the beach south of the designated bathing area. Fires must be at least 50 feet east of the sand dunes.

Concessions: There is a food and beach supply concession at each designated ocean bathing beach during the summer.

Pets: Dogs are not permitted in ocean bathing areas during the summer and must be kept on a six-foot leash at all times in other areas.

Other: Lifeguards are on duty at Bathing Units 1 and 2 from the third Saturday in June through Labor Day, daily from 10:00 A.M. to 6:00 P.M. Bathhouse rest rooms are available from May through October. Outhouses also are available.

For more information: Island Beach State Park, P.O. Box 37, Seaside Park, NJ 08752. Call 908-793-0506. To reach the nature center, call 908-793-1698.

Edwin B. Forsythe National Wildlife Refuge

If there is any advice we should offer from our summer visit to the Edwin B. Forsythe National Wildlife Refuge, it comes from the wise warning of a member of the refuge staff: "When the flag is flying, it's a good time to go outside and explore, but when it's not, you're safer behind closed doors."

You'll probably wonder what he was talking about as you approach part of the 42,000 acres of breathtaking coastal habitats, which serve as a haven for more than 250 bird species. But you won't wonder for long if you roll down your window or step outside of your car when the wind's not blowing in your favor.

The staff member was referring to the large biting fly population that thrives at the refuge during the summer, which he described as being far from your ordinary species. They're quieter, we were told, and they'll sneak right up on you.

But the biting flies serve their purpose as a food source for the tens of thousands of ducks, geese, wading birds, and shorebirds that flock to the refuge each year during the spring and fall migrations. The refuge's location along the Atlantic Flyway makes it a key link in the vast network of the more than 500 National Wildlife Refuges administered nationwide by the U.S. Fish and Wildlife Service.

The refuge system is a network of federal lands and waters selected for their value to the nation's wildlife, especially migratory birds and endangered species. A refuge differs from a park in that wildlife needs take top priority over such things as recreational activities.

The Edwin B. Forsythe National Wildlife Refuge was originally two distinct refuges: Brigantine and Barnegat. In 1984, they were combined under the Edwin B. Forsythe name in honor of the late conservationist congressman from New Jersey.

One of the primary reasons for establishing the refuge along New Jersey's coastal wetlands was to preserve the habitat and migratory routes for the Atlantic brant and American black ducks. The population of American black ducks has suffered major declines over the years. Endangered peregrine falcons also can be seen at the refuge, as well as threatened ospreys and an occasional endangered bald eagle.

Almost 90 percent of the refuge is tidal salt meadow and marsh, interspersed with shallow coves and bays. These habitats provide essential resting and feeding areas for water birds. The quiet tidal waters serve as nurseries and spawning and feeding grounds for fish and shellfish, which are important in the diets of both people and many wildlife species.

The refuge uplands also include woodlands, where trees such as pitch pines, oaks, and white cedar are common. A wide variety of wildlife species can be found in these areas, including songbirds, woodcocks, white-tailed deer, and box turtles.

More than 6,000 acres of the refuge are designated as a National Wilderness Area, including Holgate and Little Beach, two of the few remaining undeveloped barrier beaches in New Jersey. The endangered piping plover, black skimmer, and least tern can be found nesting or feeding in these areas. These birds, along with many other beach-nesting species, have suffered drastic population declines from encroaching development and loss of habitat.

In an effort to protect these rare birds and fragile natural areas, the Holgate Unit, located at the southern tip of Long Beach Island, is closed to all public use during nesting season from April 1 through August 31, and Little Beach is closed all year except by special use permit for research or education. From September 1 through March 31, the beach and tidelands of the Holgate Unit are open to public uses, including walking, surf fishing, bird-watching, photography, and nature study. Both Holgate and Little Beach Island are in the Barnegat Division.

Almost all of the refuge's public use facilities are located at the Brigantine Division headquarters in Oceanville, where an eight-mile Wildlife Drive and two short foot trails provide ideal wildlife viewing and photo opportunities.

The flag was not flying the day we visited the refuge, so the self-guiding Wildlife Drive provided the perfect opportunity to view the refuge's incredible scenery behind the recommended closed doors, as well as wading birds, such as the great and little blue herons, great and snowy egrets, and glossy ibis.

Plan to spend at least an hour on the eight-mile loop, which carries you through wetlands and uplands and affords you an ideal place to observe migratory birds and wildlife right from the roadway. We spent a good amount of time just taking in the refuge's incredible landscape, bordered by the Great, Little, and Reeds Bays.

Although refuge habitats may appear untouched, they actually are managed to support a wide variety of native plants and animals. There are 14 stops along the drive in all. With the help of a published guide available at the self-service visitor information booth, you'll be able to better understand both the refuge's diverse resources and managed activities. Two observation towers located at Gull Pond and along the drive also provide excellent places to view the surrounding wildlife.

In the midst of the natural salt marsh is the West Pool, a "freshwater oasis for wildlife." Fresh water is a critical resource in the salt marsh environment for many bird species, which fly in daily from nearby salt bays to drink and wash salt residues from their feathers.

The 900-acre West Pool reflects the important management strategy of diking. Through the use of water control structures along the dikes, water levels are controlled and are periodically changed to produce abundant wildlife food plants on the muddy bottom. The West Pool interior is also diked, creating two freshwater habitats that can be managed independently for greater diversity. By creating freshwater pools in the salt marsh, a more diverse and abundant variety of birds and other wildlife is supported.

Another important area essential to creating the refuge's diverse landscape is the East Pool, a 700-acre impoundment containing shallow brackish water. The pool contains a mixture of saltwater and freshwater, which support a variety of invertebrates important in the diets of many shorebirds. Sandpipers and plovers can be seen along the muddy edges of both pools from August through early September.

Two short walking loops through the refuge's uplands, including a boardwalk adjacent to the marshlands, are available for visitors to explore on foot otherwise inaccessible areas.

Where: The Brigantine Division of the Edwin B. Forsythe National Wildlife Refuge can be reached directly off U.S. 9, south of the town of Smithville. Follow marker signs to Great Creek Road. The Barnegat Division is located east of U.S. 9.
Hours: The refuge is open daily from sunrise to sunset. An information office and auditorium are located in the refuge headquarters building in the Brigantine Division. The office is open weekdays from 8:00 A.M. to 4:00 P.M. year-round.
Admission: $3.00-per-vehicle entrance fees are in effect daily at the Brigantine Division. When a fee collector is not on duty, visitors must pay at self-serve payment sites. Disabled individuals or those who are 62 years of age or older may apply in person to receive a free lifetime entrance pass. Children under 16 are admitted free.
Best time to visit: The best wildlife viewing occurs in spring and fall.
Activities: Seasonal waterfowl and deer hunting, fishing, and crabbing are permitted in designated areas of both the Brigantine and Barnegat divisions.
Concessions: None.

Pets: Pets must be on a short, handheld leash in all areas of the Brigantine Division. Pets are prohibited at Holgate.

Other: Organized groups should contact the refuge and register their visits in advance. Wildlife Drive brochures, bird checklists, and information on seasonal wildlife activity are available at the refuge office. Biting insects abound from mid-May through September. Insect repellent is recommended.

For more information: Edwin B. Forsythe National Wildlife Refuge, Great Creek Road, P.O. Box 72, Oceanville, NJ 08231. Call 609-652-1665.

Marine Mammal Stranding Center

When an animal is sick, you call a veterinarian. But what if you spot a sick dolphin or whale, or maybe a lost seal? Who will respond then?

In New Jersey, it's the Marine Mammal Stranding Center, a nonprofit organization that was formed in 1978 by a handful of volunteers. Based in Brigantine, the center has answered more than 1,700 calls for stranded whales, dolphins, seals, and sea turtles that have washed ashore on New Jersey beaches. They range from a 5-pound Kemp's ridley sea turtle to a 25-ton humpback whale, both of which are endangered species.

The causes of strandings vary. The animals can be injured through accidental nettings by commercial fishing operations, through collisions with boats and ships, or through shark attacks. Other animals become entangled in polypropylene and monofilament fishing lines or plastic six-pack rings. Parasites or other health problems can cause animals to become ill or disoriented, while younger animals, such as seals, can easily become lost.

As northern waters become extremely cold in the winter, seals migrate south, some as far as North Carolina. While in New Jersey, seals often come out of the water to dry and warm themselves in the sun or to avoid rough seas. A seal that comes out of the water is said to have "hauled out." Beaches, jetties, and docks are possible haul-out sites. Stranded seals also haul out, but they may not go back into the water.

When we visited the center in September, a stranded 14-month-old harp seal was resting quietly in a 12,000-gallon indoor tank during its second appearance in a year at the facility. The previous spring, the malnourished seal had hauled out off the coast of New Jersey. It soon found itself in the care of the Marine Mammal Stranding Center, where staffers nursed it back to health and finally released it off the coast. Six months later, however, the seal hauled out again north of Brigantine.

Robert Schoelkopf, the center's director, speculated that the seal might have spent six months swimming and then hauled out to rest. It appeared to be healthy this time but was attracting so much attention from curious onlookers that the center "rescued" the seal out of fear that it might bite someone or be hurt. When we visited, the center was in the process of trying to arrange for a new home for the seal up north where it belonged, as well as the transportation there. Shortly after we visited, the seal was flown to Canada and released at Sable Island, 150 miles from Nova Scotia.

Stranded seals can be very dangerous, so they should not be approached. As for whales or dolphins, the federal Marine Mammal Protection Act prohibits purposely coming closer than 100 feet in the wild. Conscientious ship captains who offer sightseeing trips to see dolphins and whales off the Jersey coast are careful to keep a safe distance away from these animals. But you don't have to take a sightseeing tour to get a good look at them. Just sit on the beach and wait. In the summer, you can spot humpback whales off southern New Jersey, while bottle-nosed dolphins can be spotted from central New Jersey southward from May to September.

The center, which is supported solely by membership fees and donations, is the only organization authorized to rescue and rehabilitate stranded marine mammals and sea turtles in New Jersey. When you visit, you can tour the center's small museum and take a look at any rescued animals that may be in the holding tanks at the time. And if you're like us, you'll sign up as members before you leave so that this worthwhile effort can continue.

Where: The Marine Mammal Stranding Center is located in Brigantine. Follow the Atlantic City Expressway, Garden State Parkway, or U.S. 30 or County 40 east into Atlantic City. Follow signs for Trump Marina and Harrah's Casino. Take Brigantine Bridge (between Harrah's and Trump Marina) into Brigantine. The Marine Mammal Stranding Center is on the left, two miles from the top of the bridge and 100 yards before Lighthouse Circle.

Hours: The center is open weekends from noon to 4:00 P.M. for tours. From mid-June to Labor Day, the center is open daily from 11:00 A.M. to 5:00 P.M.

Admission: $1.00 donation.

Best time to visit: Year-round.

Activities: The center offers educational cruises and trips during the summer. Call for more information.

Concessions: A gift shop sells T-shirts, sweatshirts, books, and other items related to marine animals.

Other: Membership fees are $15.00 for individuals and $25.00 for families.

For more information: Marine Mammal Stranding Center, P.O. Box 773, Brigantine, NJ 08203. Call 609-266-0538.

The Wetlands Institute

New Jersey has made a great effort to save its endangered freshwater and saltwater wetlands from encroaching development, and the Wetlands Institute, located in Stone Harbor, provides a place for the public to get up close to these impressive coastal ecosystems and gain a new respect for their continued existence.

Nearly half of New Jersey's 245,000 acres of salt marsh are found along the Delaware Bay and the Atlantic coast of Cape May, Atlantic, and Ocean Counties. The salt marshes surrounding the institute are typical of those throughout the state.

Twenty of the more than 50 animal species on New Jersey's lists of endangered and threatened wildlife are directly dependent on freshwater wetlands. The wetlands provide the only available nursery areas for many of these animals, including the endangered blue-spotted salamander and bog turtle, as well as the great blue heron, considered to be threatened in New Jersey.

Wetlands plants help absorb urban pollution and control flooding and soil erosion caused by such natural occurrences as spring snow melt and intense rains. They also provide food sources for many animals year-round, including deer, bears, and other large mammals.

It was not until the state Coastal Wetlands Act of 1970 that the value of these productive and essential ecosystems was recognized and they were protected. Before then, many people viewed wetlands as mere swamps and useless marshes.

The Wetlands Institute is a private, nonprofit organization dedicated to the continued research of these endangered ecosystems and to educating the public through a wide variety of educational programs, tours, and exhibits for both adults and children.

The institute's buildings include classrooms, an exhibit and lecture hall, an observation tower, six research laboratories, a library, and a museum, all surrounded by acres of publicly owned salt marsh and an award-winning garden of native seashore plants. The marsh and nearby upland and barrier island habitats serve as outdoor classrooms.

The institute was founded in 1969 by Herbert H. Mills, a conservationist who was concerned about the alarming widespread loss of coastal wetlands. At that time, there were no laws regulating wetlands use. In an effort to curb the loss, Mills raised funds to purchase 6,000 acres of wetlands. The acreage later was purchased by the state of New Jersey.

A spectacular view of the diverse wetlands landscape of grassy meadows and circling birds can be seen from the institute's observation tower. We almost missed this sight, however, as we debated whether to make the steep climb up the narrow spiral steps that led the way to the lookout. We summoned up our courage, however, and the view was worth the climb. A young artist was sketching the osprey nest visible from the tower, and several people were peering through binoculars at the panoramic view.

We got a closer look at the nesting osprey from Marshview Hall, a meeting room located just downstairs from the tower, featuring wildlife art and floor-to-ceiling windows overlooking the marshes. Two telescopes were set up by the staff and pointed directly at the nest, providing a breathtaking, up-close view.

Located just around the corner from Marshview Hall is Wetlandia, a children's discovery room with games and exhibits.

Outside the main building is a boardwalk where we followed tiny, etched bird footprints to the entrance of Secrets of the Salt Marsh, the institute's adjacent museum. Exhibits explain the wetlands food web and the important role that each and every species living in the wetlands plays. For example, mosquitoes and other insects are important because they are food for birds and fish (a lesson you'll come to appreciate fully as they accompany you along the self-guided trail).

The museum also features an aquarium with live seahorses and puffer fish, as well as a discovery table with microscopes where children can explore for themselves some of the species that live in the wetlands. In the touch tank, children can hold whelks—shells that house large sea snails—which are often found resting in the shallow waters along the shore.

A marked salt marsh trail guides you through the diverse natural habitats surrounding the institute. This is a great place for bird-watching and learning the different plant species common to marshlands.

There are 13 stops in all, each familiarizing you with different common sights afforded by the wetlands landscape, such as Spartina grasses, bayberry shrubs, and slender-leaved goldenrod.

During the summer, bird-watchers often can see boat-tailed grackles and red-winged blackbirds guarding their nesting areas. Species of waterfowl and other birds feed and nest in the surrounding bays, channels, and tidal marshes, where they can best be seen during their fall and spring migrations.

June and July are terrapin nesting season. Keep your eyes open for adult female terrapins emerging from the marsh creeks to lay their eggs on the higher ground. You should also watch your step! Young terrapins about the size of a quarter might be crawling about from the previous summer. These young turtles, mostly seen during March and April, probably were hatched too late in the fall to head for open water, and rather than risk the cold, they spent the winter underground.

Where: The Wetlands Institute is located in Middle Township. From the Garden State Parkway, take Exit 10. Proceed east on Stone Harbor Boulevard for three miles. The institute is on the right before Stone Harbor Bridge.

Hours: The institute is open Monday through Saturday from 9:30 A.M. to 4:30 P.M., and Sunday from 10:00 A.M. to 4:00 P.M. from May 15 through October 15. For the remainder of the year, it's open Tuesday through Saturday from 9:30 A.M. to 4:30 P.M. and is closed on Sunday and Monday.

Admission: $3.00 for adults, $2.00 for children under 12.

Best time to visit: The fall and spring bird migration seasons are the best times to visit. However, with the ever-changing character of the wetlands landscape, any time is a good time to visit. Birders, bring your binoculars!

Activities: Educational programs and field trips offered include summer nature classes for children, special preschool classes, guided salt marsh safaris, bird expeditions, a year-round public lecture series, family "creature days," natural history courses, student internships, films and videotape programs, boat trips, and adult workshops, including carving, art, quilting, and photography.

Concessions: A gift shop is located just as you enter the institute's main building. Handcrafted gifts, T-shirts, jewelry, books, and other gifts all have nature-related themes.

Other: The institute annually sponsors the "Wings 'n Water Festival," a popular event occurring the third weekend in September. National decoy and carving shows and wildlife art are two of the festival's main attractions.

For more information: The Wetlands Institute, 1075 Stone Harbor Boulevard, Stone Harbor, NJ 08247. Call 609-368-1211.

Cape May Birding

There's no doubt about it: Cape May is a birder's paradise. Considered one of the top birding hot spots in all of North America, Cape May, located at the southernmost tip of New Jersey, provides a crucial resting and feeding place for migrant birds before they cross Delaware Bay. And when the birds converge on Cape May, so do the birders.

Shorebirds winter in South America and then travel to the Arctic tundra to breed in June. On their journey between these locations, they need a refueling spot that will provide them with ample food. They find this on Delaware Bay in the form of the eggs of more than a million horseshoe crabs using the beaches to spawn. The tens of thousands of these birds, including the red knot, ruddy turnstone, semipalmated sandpiper, sanderling, dunlin, and short-billed dowitcher, are a sight to behold as they converge on Reed's Beach for a few weeks each year from early May to early June to feast on the horseshoe crabs.

In the fall, hawks such as bald eagles, peregrine falcons, ospreys, and red-tailed and broad-winged hawks travel south to Cape May, where they hunt and rest in the surrounding forests before crossing Delaware Bay on their way to spend the winter in the southeastern United States and Central and South America.

Cape May also hosts more than 200 species of songbirds, including warblers and sparrows, that pass through on the way to their wintering grounds in Central and South America. In addition, thousands of migrating monarch butterflies pass through on their journey to Central America.

To find out what birds have been spotted in the area prior to your visit, call or stop in at the New Jersey Audubon Society's Cape May Bird Observatory. Here, you can pick up birding maps, a bird checklist, and other related material. You also can call the Cape May Birding Hotline at 609-861-0466 for a recorded listing of rare bird sightings from South Jersey, as well as general and natural history information.

If you're a beginning bird-watcher, Cape May Point State Park is an ideal place to start. Although both spring and fall migrations occur, fall generally is considered the best time to see songbirds, shorebirds, and hawks, as well as waterfowl. The park features a raised platform that provides excellent views of the freshwater marsh and of the migrating hawks as they fly down the coastline. The best time to see the hawks fill the sky is from mid-September through October.

The Cape May Bird Observatory conducts an annual hawk watch here, and it's not unusual for more than 1,000 hawks to be spotted in one day. Keeping track of the migrating birds is an official hawk counter who staffs the platform and will point out the more unusual species, such as peregrines.

While Cape May Point State Park is known for hawks, songbirds are the main attraction at the Higbee Beach Wildlife Management Area. Its 886 acres contain several different types of habitat, including fields, wooded areas, freshwater ponds, a jetty, 1.5 miles of beach, freshwater meadows, and dunes.

Millions of songbirds migrate through this area annually, and if you visit between late August and October, it's not unusual to find the parking lots here full of cars at dawn. That's when birders are out in force to see large numbers of songbirds flying into the area seeking refuge in the fields and forests. Hawks can be spotted here, too, with more than 50,000 migrating through the area every year.

Where: Cape May Point State Park is located at the tip of Cape May, about four miles from the end of the Garden State

Parkway. Located on Lighthouse Avenue, it is accessible via Sunset Boulevard.

Higbee Beach is accessible from New England Road on the north side, and Sunset Boulevard on the south and is approximately 4.5 miles from the southern end of the Garden State Parkway.

The Cape May Bird Observatory is on East Lake Drive, off Lighthouse Avenue.

Reed's Beach is located off State 47 on Reed's Beach Road, about 5.5 miles south of State 83.

Hours: Cape May Point State Park is open daily from dawn to dusk. The visitors center is open daily 8:00 A.M. to 8:00 P.M. in summer, Sunday through Thursday 9:00 A.M. to 4:00 P.M. and Friday and Saturday 8:00 A.M. to 6:00 P.M. in spring and fall, Wednesday through Sunday 9:00 A.M. to 4:00 P.M. in winter.

The Cape May Bird Observatory is open daily from 10:00 A.M. to 5:00 P.M.

Higbee Beach is open daily from dawn to dusk.

Admission: All of the abovementioned areas are free.

Best time to visit: Spring and fall.

Activities: Cape May Point State Park has more than three miles of trails and boardwalks in its natural area, offering many excellent nature study and hiking opportunities. The park also has a half-mile self-guiding nature trail, which is wheelchair-accessible.

Higbee Beach also is used for fishing, nature walking, and hunting. It's a popular spot to look for "Cape May Diamonds," smooth quartz pebbles that can resemble diamonds when cut and polished.

The Cape May Bird Observatory offers educational lectures; year-round activities, such as bird identification walks; field trips; and spring and autumn weekend packages. It also conducts hawk-banding demonstrations in September and

October at the hawk-watch platform in Cape May Point State Park, providing excellent opportunities to see these birds up close.

Concessions: Cape May Point State Park's visitors center sells nature books and postcards. Souvenirs also are sold at the lighthouse. The Cape May Bird Observatory has a store featuring books, optics, and educational materials.

Pets: Pets at Cape May Point State Park must be on a six-foot maximum leash and under control.

Other: Cape May Point State Park brochures are available in the visitors center, which also houses a museum featuring the natural and cultural heritage of the Cape May region. Picnic facilities are available. You may tour the lighthouse here for a small fee.

Bird-watching at Higbee Beach is restricted to designated trails from September 15 through November 1. During that time, group size is limited to six people or fewer, except by non-fee permit available at the Higbee Beach office. Fall visitors must remain on maintained trails. From Memorial Day to Labor Day, only one parking lot is open, located one mile from the beach on New England Road. Beware of possible nudity; nudists frequent the beach during the summer. Refer to the bulletin board in the parking lot for regulations in effect during your visit.

Much of the Reed's Beach area is private property, so limit your viewing to the platform and jetty.

For more information: Cape May Point State Park, P.O. Box 107, Cape May Point, NJ 08212. Call 609-884-2159. Higbee Beach Wildlife Management Area, Division of Fish, Game and Wildlife, P.O. Box 400, Trenton, NJ 08625. Call 609-629-0090. Cape May Bird Observatory, P.O. Box 3, Cape May Point, NJ 08212. Call 609-884-2736.

Index